OUR BLESSED MOTHER

OUR LADY OF HELP.

*Reproduced by kind permission of Rt. Rev. Mgr. C. Corbishley, M.A.,
President, Ushaw College, Durham.*

OUR BLESSED MOTHER

Talks on Our Lady

by

EDWARD LEEN, C.S.Sp.

and

JOHN KEARNEY, C.S.Sp.

P. J. KENEDY & SONS

NEW YORK

DE LICENTIA SUPERIORUM

D. Murphy, C.S.Sp., Praep.Prov.Hib.

Dublini, die 11 Octobris, 1946.

NIHIL OBSTAT:

Michael L. Dempsey
Censor Theol. Deput.

IMPRIMI POTEST:

✠ Ioannes Carolus
Archiep : Dublinen.,
Hiberniae Primas

Dublini, die 27 Octobris 1946

CONTENTS

DEDICATION

To the Immaculate Virgin
The Glory of Jerusalem
The Joy of Israel
The Honour of Our People
Whom
In the Present Crisis of Human History
The Church salutes
as

"THE HOPE OF THE WORLD"

" O Blessed Virgin Mary, Thou who art the Mother of Grace, and the Hope of the World, hear us thy children, crying unto Thee."

(Antiphon for Lauds: Office of the Feast of the Immaculate Heart of Mary).

FOREWORD.

For many years I was intimately associated with two beloved confrères—Dr. Edward Leen and Fr. John Kearney—and after their deaths, it was my duty to collect their papers. In the discharge of this office it was borne in upon me that it would be only fitting to give the thoughts of these two saintly priests on Our Blessed Lady to the English speaking world. Besides, since it is evident that the reign of Our Blessed Lady is to be the character of the spirituality of the coming time, it occurred to me that I should make this contribution to Marian devotion.

In the case of Dr. Leen, there was a special reason for publishing this series of his talks. In the biographical sketches that appeared in the press after his death it was stated that when God called him to his reward he was engaged on a work on Our Lady. As a result of this statement, countless enquiries have been addressed to members of the Congregation of the Holy Ghost, asking when the book on Our Lady would appear. Many perhaps, will be disappointed when, as his literary executor, I inform them that Dr. Leen has left no MSS of such a work. In fact, it is true to say that he has *written* nothing on Our Blessed Lady except what has already been published in *The True Vine and Its Branches* and *In the Likeness of Christ*. Nevertheless, Dr. Leen had contemplated writing a book on Our Blessed Lady, and was already forming, in his own mind, the plan of such a book. One day, not long before his unexpected death, when discussing certain literary projects, he said to me with great earnestness: "If I could write a book on Our Blessed Lady, I should feel that my work as a spiritual writer would be complete." But God, in His inscrutable designs, called Dr. Leen to Himself, before that desire could be realised.

The Chapters in the first section of this book give at least a glimpse of the thoughts about Our Blessed Lady that were uppermost in Dr. Leen's mind, and so they are the best attempt that can be made to give the public what they were expecting but can never obtain. They are *talks* given by Dr. Leen on different occasions, and were never *written* by him. For their content I am indebted very largely to the notes taken by the Sisters of the Holy Rosary, Killeshandra, when Dr. Leen spoke to them about Our Blessed Lady. Owing to the system adopted, we can be sure that they are an authentic record of Dr. Leen's words. Certain Sisters were deputed to take down his words in shorthand; after the Conferences, these Sisters compared and checked up the results of their efforts. Such is the origin of the contents of the present work.

This book is, then, in a " *genre* " quite different from Dr. Leen's other works. In those other works his genius as a literary craftsman appears. These *talks,* given at different times to different audiences and without any thought of subsequent publication, may lack the literary finish, the logical sequence and orderly development that should characterise a written treatise, but they are instinct with the warm earnestness, the spontaneity and eager tones of a true Apostle of Our Blessed Lady. Thus they have a special value. In the frequent iteration of the main theme—the reality of Mary's Motherhood—appears the maturity, completeness and simplicity of spiritual vision which constitutes Dr. Leen's fundamental claim to greatness as a spiritual writer.

I have added to the *talks* by Dr. Leen, four chapters on the Immaculate Heart of Mary, that had been given as conferences to various audiences, by Fr. Kearney. It is truly remarkable that this saintly friend and colleague of Dr. Leen was also contemplating as a last work, a book on Our Blessed Lady, with the title—" Devotion to the Immaculate Heart." But in his case too, God called him to his eternal reward before he could give effect to his holy desire.

Both of these writers were ardent lovers of Our Lady. Both desired to make her better known and loved. Both felt how inadequate would be their best attempts. In this connection it is of interest to note a statement made by Dr. Leen in the course of a conference given just a few months before his death: "I believe, God will raise up a Saint who will teach us the place and the influence of Mary on our supernatural life. This, it appears to me will be the consummation of Christianity. No one, so far as I know, has yet *fully* elucidated her role, her true motherhood of our whole spiritual life. I have tried to write about her myself in the last few chapters of *The True Vine and Its Branches,* but the result is far short of my desires and I know that much remains yet to be said of the practical action of Mary in every human soul."

In these words of Dr. Leen, I seem to hear an echo of the words attributed to St. Thomas Aquinas, who, when asked on his death-bed, to expound the Canticle of Canticles, answered " Give me the spirit of St. Bernard and I shall do what you ask."

As to Fr. Kearney, from my intimate knowledge of him, I can say that to him were applicable the words of St. Bernard himself: "I have long felt a wish to write something in order to satisfy my devotion to the Mother of God, but the multiplicity of my occupations prevented me from doing it."

There is a peculiar element of pathos in the appeal of a posthumous work. This pathetic note is deepened when one realises that the authors were already nearing the eternal shore at the time when some of the thoughts contained in the present collection of *talks* on Our Blessed Lady, were expressed. These pages may be regarded as a wreath laid on the tomb of two departed friends in a sincere, but inadequate attempt to give effect to their holy wish of communicating to the world, their thoughts on Our Lady. May these *talks* help to prolong in the coming time, the beneficent and widespread effects of the apostolate exercised by them, through written and spoken word.

I must not, however, conclude this foreword without expressing the debt of deep gratitude that I owe to Sr. Mary Laurence and her co-workers of St. Mary's Convent, Arklow, for their most generous and devoted help, as well as for many valuable constructive suggestions; to Rev. M. J. Troy, C.S.Sp., Rev. G. Gibbons, C.S.Sp., the theological students of the House of Studies at Kimmage, for their painstaking and unselfish assistance in reading critically both the MSS and the proofs.

May the Heart of Our Immaculate Mother reward all who

contributed to show the deep wisdom contained in those beautiful words of St. Bernard:

" Studeamus per Mariam ascendere ad Christum, qui per ipsam descendit ad nos."

" Let us strive, through Mary, to ascend to Christ, Who, through her descended to us."

BERNARD FENNELLY,
Holy Ghost College,
Kimmage,
Dublin.

FEAST OF THE PURIFICATION, 1946.

ACKNOWLEDGEMENTS.

The Literary Editor wishes to make grateful acknowledgement of the very kind and gracious permission of the Superioress General of the Holy Rosary Sisters, Killeshandra, to use freely the notes taken by members of the Community, in order to reproduce and publish these *talks* of him who may be aptly called the Co-Founder and Spiritual Father of this now flourishing Missionary Congregation.

He also gladly avails of this occasion to thank Messrs Sheed and Ward (London), and also the firm of P. J. Kenedy and Sons (New York), for having graciously allowed him to reproduce, if he deemed it desirable, the Chapters concerning Our Blessed Lady in the works of Dr. Leen published by them: [*In the Likeness of Christ,* (Sheed and Ward); *The True Vine and Its Branches* (P. J. Kenedy & Sons).]

At first it was intended to avail of their kind offer, but on consideration it was thought preferable to confine the work to the merely *spoken* word of Dr. Leen.

Readers, however, may note that Dr. Leen in some of his talks reproduced almost verbally some passages in the above mentioned works. This is not to be wondered at. Dr. Leen had often to speak about Our Lady without much time for preparation. On such occasions, it is probable that instinctively he expressed himself in language that he had already used when writing about Our Blessed Lady. On the other hand, it may have happened that some of the notes taken by the Sisters at Holy Rosary Convent, Killeshandra, were given to him, and that later on, when writing the Chapters on Our Blessed Lady in the above mentioned works, he utilized, while perfecting from a literary point of view, the expression of his spoken word. And so in a twofold way we may say that in these *talks* we have " nova et vetera " by Dr. Leen concerning Our Blessed Lady.

Thanks are due also to the Manager of the Spiritual Book Associates, Inc. (New York), for his kind permission to reproduce the Chapter on " Mother and Child," which Dr. Leen gave as a lecture during his tour in America in 1939, and which was published by the firm in a work called *The Mother of God.*

CHAPTER I.

THE NEW EVE

" And she brought forth her first-born Son " (Luke ii. 7).

GOD HAS ONE ONLY-BEGOTTEN SON by nature. By grace He has called a multitude to participate in the Divine Sonship, and thus become His children, so that the Son of God " might be the first-born amongst many brethern." The Divine Word, the Second Person of the Blessed Trinity, become incarnate, is the Only-begotten of Mary according to His Human nature. He is the only child born of her physically, the only being to whom she communicated her most pure flesh and blood. Jesus was the Only-begotten of the Father according to Divine generation. He was the Only-begotten of Mary according to human generation. But in His earthly, as in His heavenly birth, He was to be the first-born of a multitude of others. Mary is Mother of Jesus according to the flesh; she is Mother according to the spirit of all those who by grace are made comformable to His image. In the supernatural order all christians have God for their Father, deriving from Him their supernatural life and being. In the same supernatural realm, they have for their Mother, Mary, through whom that life is transmitted. We are born of God and we are born of Mary. Mary is, in very truth, the Mother of our supernatural life.

In a most true sense it is from Mary that the regenerated human race takes its origin. In God's design man was created for the purpose of repairing the losses caused by the fall of the Angels. To the angelic spirits God had given a participation in His own life and His own nature. The wonderful faculties and powers that belong to their existence, magnificent as they were, had value in the eyes of God, only as being the basis on which was to be constructed the spiritual edifice of the supernatural life. In the case of mankind, the natural existence which in virtue of their creation men enjoyed, was, in God's plan merely the condition of the possibility of meriting the communication of His own inner life and being. Thus human

1

life, considered in itself, counted for nothing in the eyes of God, but human life dignified and renewed, elevated and transformed by the impression of the Divine Life, was contemplated by Him with infinite complacency. Man's life, thus env,saged, is for God, a beautiful earthly visage of His own Divine perfections. The angels in grace were a beautiful celestial mirror; men in grace an earthly one in which were reproduced the Divine features of the God-head. By sin that reflection was shattered. Angelic and human life as the result of sin lost all its value. It ceased to be life and became as death. Eve had been created by God to be the fountain from which was to issue that unending stream of supernatural life, which was to flow in all her children, making them sons of God, and citizens of heaven, whilst being denizens of the earth. The destiny of Eve was a dazzling one. Because of her fall, we are apt to forget the glory that was to be hers. She was meant to be a living fountain, not merely of natural, but of supernatural life; her soul was created immaculate in order that her race should be stainless. By an act of disobedience she defiled the stream at its source. Dead herself, she could transmit nothing but death. In her the human race was, as it were, stillborn. It, as far as God was concerned, ceased to exist. She, who was to be the mother of the living, had become the mother of the dead.

God determined to create anew. There was no hesitation, no delay. By one woman the race had found death, by another it was to be restored to life. A fresh fountain of supernatural earthly existence had to be created. The Lord said to the serpent: " I will put enmities between thee and the woman, and thy seed and her seed : she shall crush thy head and thou shalt lie in wait for her heel." (Gen. iii. 15.) Thus was enunciated the decree of the Immaculate Conception, and thus was inaugurated a new order. The first Adam and the first Eve passed out of their position in the supernatural order, and were replaced by the new Adam and the new Eve. Mary, ' the Woman ' enters on her sublime destiny. As the new Eve, she will be the transmitter of life Divine to all her children.

Mary was created the new mother of the human race. The first Eve was formed of the first Man. Now the order is reversed ; the New Adam is to be born of the New Eve. The position thus given to Mary is dazzling in its sublimity. From her we see issuing, in orderly procession, first Jesus Christ, and then, during all the succeeding ages, those who were, by the merits of the Passion, to share in the Life of which He has the plenitude. Mary seems to be the beginning of all things; and she would have been the beginning were it not that she was incapable of meriting that first Grace which was the source of her dignity. It was the Passion of Jesus that merited for Mary that full flood of Divine Life which was poured into her soul at the moment that it issued immaculate from the creative Hands of God. Mary was the source of redemption, but she, too, needed to be redeemed. She needed preservation from the condition that was naturally hers, through being one of the race of her who was the Mother of the Dead. Mary's soul was not first formed and then sanctified. Mary's soul was sanctified at its formation. There was no priority, no succession in these two processes of formation and sanctification. Such was the Immaculate Conception. Mary was redeemed, but the Redemption of the race was not yet accomplished. This initial grace of Mary's Immaculate Conception was but the dawning of the salvation and the redemption of mankind. In logical priority the infusion of Divine Life into Mary's soul was the first return of God to His own creation, after He had been banished from it by the disobedience of our First Parents. As an act of disobedience had banished Him, an act of obedience and submission was to recall Him. For fifteen years Mary, in her own person, comprised all God's world. Outside of and around that simple Jewish maiden, the world wheeled its flight, a lost world. She was the only living thing in a vast realm of dead. God, looking from Heaven on the generations of men, was confronted everywhere with thick darkness, and in that darkness there stood out only one beacon of light. That beacon was Mary. The Life of God that was in Mary burned more brightly every moment. At each instant the worship of her soul, its profound and humble subjection to its Creator fulfilled the conditions that enabled God to give her the fullest participation in His Life that it was possible, in the order of Providence, for Him to give. Not the slightest faltering in her soul deflected the continuous stream that poured on her from the Fountains of the Divinity. At each instant her receptivity was at its highest, because her correspondence was perfect. The beauty and magnificence of her soul attained wondrous perfections. St. Leo says of her that her grace became so great, her realisation of and her union with God so sublime that she, as it were, brought Christ to birth in her mind before He was born of her in Bethlehem.

The world was prepared for God's return, but in His all-wise designs, God would re-enter His world only with the consent of His creatures. God is of wondrous delicacy in His dealings with us; He stands at the door of our souls, waits for us, if we will, to open to Him. He never employs force or constraint. For the second time, the destiny of the human race turned on a woman's word. Our first Mother heard the false angel's suggestion, and in her pride said: " I will be as God." Mary, our second Mother, the New Eve, hears the message of Gabriel, and from the depths of her humility utters her *Ecce ancilla Domini*. The pride of one woman caused our ruin: the humility of another brings about our restoration. With the consent of Mary to the Divine proposal, the Redemption had begun. The Incarnation had taken place. " The Word was made flesh and dwelt amongst us."[1] God returns to His own creation. The human race has a Saviour.

Mary might well have hesitated. It was not so much a privilege that she was asked to accept, as a sacrifice of appalling proportions that she was asked to make. She was summoned to be the Mother of God, Who was to be a Saviour. His name was to be Jesus, and His Mission was to be that of a Redeemer. Mary was being called upon to leave the calm and peace of the life she had been leading for fifteen years, in order to enter into, and take part in, the fierce strife of the Redemption. A world of tears and blood and of stupendous suffering spread before her. No wonder her great soul was shaken to its depths, though her strong will never wavered. God's gifts are terrible in what they exact from nature. Mary knew sufficiently well, though not yet with an absolute distinctness, what her rôle of Motherhood

[1] John i. 14.

involved. That rôle was to become clearer as time went on, but there was never a moment in which she was in doubt as to what God demanded of her. The shadow of Calvary lay heavy over the manger in which she laid her First-born; it was to envelope her completely and in agonies of pain, when she was to bring us forth, her other children, re-created by the Blood of her First-born. When Gabriel's words fell upon her senses, Mary realised that she would have to make the utter sacrifice of all her being. In the supreme moment of her 'Fiat,' she knew that her soul would be searched with pain to its utmost depths, and that the instrument of her torture would be her creature-love of God, sublimated and exalted, enriched and refined by the overwhelmingly tender infusion of maternal love. She foresaw that she was to be lifted up on high in order to be plunged into unfathomable abysses of pain. Her own *co-passion* mingling with her Son's Passion, loomed menacingly before her mental gaze. She bowed her head and consented to be the Co-Redemptrix of the human race; to be not only the Mother of Christ, but also the Mother of Christians; to give birth, not only to Jesus, but also to Jesus' mystical members.

It was a glorious thing to bring forth into the world the Son of God Himself—to clothe Him in flesh and blood. It was a wonderful privilege to be the source of the human, physical life of Jesus Christ. But it must be remembered that Jesus did not come to gladden men by the fair aspect of His human nature and the beauty of His human acts, but to impart to them that soul-life of which His human acts were the material expression. "I am come that they may have life, and may have it more abundantly."[2] His physical birth was a means, not an end. It was simply a means to the spiritual birth of man. So too was Mary's physical maternity. The rôle of her spiritual maternity, Mary, from the first moment of her 'Fiat,' had clearly envisaged and embraced, but Simeon's terrible prophecy sounded, for her, the depths of her sacrifice and revealed, with startling lucidity, the co-redeeming part she was to play in the salvation of mankind. Bethlehem was but a prelude to Calvary. Jesus' mission and hers began in the Cave but reached their consummation only on Calvary.

[2] John x. 10.

For Jesus and Mary the Cross was final, all else led up to it as a foreshadowing or preparation. For the world was born anew only at the moment of the Crucifixion; it was only then that men became definitely the brothers of Jesus Christ and the children of Mary. The Passion of Our Lord gave us the Immaculate Conception, and from the Immaculate Conception Mary has come to the Motherhood of God. Our Divine Lord's human life was the first gift of Mary to men, and with that life were given all the graces destined to issue from it and, in the present order of Providence, there is no grace that does not issue therefrom. Mary is therefore the Mother of Grace. It is she who brings to birth all those that live by the life of grace. It is she who transmits the Redemption that was won for us by Jesus Christ. In the original plan, Eve was to have been the transmitter of that Supernatural Life which was imparted to her gratuitously by God from the beginning. Mary in the new order of things, is the Fountain from which comes to us that same supernatural life that was merited and secured for us by the death of her Divine Son.

Mary is really and truly Our Mother in the supernatural order. God's angel was the messenger of the first Annunciation by which she was proclaimed the Mother of God. God's own Son was the herald of the second Annunciation by which she was hailed the Mother of mankind. The first was a prelude to the second. The circumstances in which the two announcements were made were widely different. Gabriel spoke to Mary in the calm peace of her home in Nazareth whilst she was absorbed in deep prayer; Jesus addressed her from the height of the Cross whilst the tumult of men's passions, inflamed by Hell, raged in a storm of fury around her. " When Jesus therefore had seen His Mother and the disciple standing whom he loved, he saith to his mother: Woman, Behold thy Son. After that, he saith to the disciple: Behold thy Mother."[3] In these words the Evangelist relates an event which marks an epoch in the world's history. From the Cross the spiritual Maternity of the New Eve is proclaimed to mankind, and Our Mother Mary, in one powerful out-flow of the most tender love, embraces and enfolds in her maternal care, the children of God.

[3] John xix. 27.

The words of Jesus "Behold Thy Mother" are not a command. They are just as were the words of Gabriel in Nazareth a request; and now on Calvary, Mary renews her "Ecce ancilla Domini," and consummates the offering of Jesus made by her in the Temple forty days after His birth. She united her will absolutely with the Divine Will; she repeated His prayer in the Garden; she accepted to will, in spite of the cost, the Redemption of mankind. Utterly forgetful of self, and in a sublime sacrifice of creature-love and Mother-love Mary accepted and offered up to God, for the Redemption of mankind, the death of her Divine Son upon the Cross. The making of this act of sacrifice rent her soul with agony, and in that agony we, her children, were brought to our spiritual birth. Her First-Born was brought forth painlessly; we, her other children, were brought forth in intolerable anguish. Mary's acceptance on Calvary of her spiritual Motherhood was the final act in the restoration of men. She consented that Jesus should die. Mary laid on the altar of the Cross all the tender instincts of a perfect Mother's heart. Uniting her will with the Divine Will, she renews at the foot of the Cross, the perfect oblation already made by her at Nazareth when she uttered her sublime prayer "Ecce ancilla Domini."

"From that hour the disciple took her to his own."[4] Our Lord's words, "Behold thy Mother" conditioned by Mary's consent, effect what they signify. At her acceptance, there was created in her heart, for us her children, a love of surpassing depth, possessing all the tenderness and devotedness of maternal affection. She was not only named, she became in fact a mother to each one of us, bearing towards us all a mother's love. In John and in all those of whom he is the type and representative, these same words produced a correlative effect. They touched and opened up in him all those well-springs of filial affection, which abound in the heart of a devoted son for the best and most perfect of mothers. No one can be a true brother to Jesus Christ without entertaining a child's love towards Mary. One who cannot look upon her, and look to her instinctively as a mother, has not a true Christian spirit. He does not fully belong to Christ's family. Christ's words, spoken from the Cross, have not reached him.

[4] John xix. 27.

Mary, in her rôle of mother towards us, fosters, protects and nurtures the life infused into our souls by God, Our Father. Its development is entrusted to her maternal care. It is her function to protect us against all the dangers that surround us. Mary is our Mother and treats us with all the tenderness of a Mother's love, attending to and supplying all our needs. An incessant flow of actual grace is necessary for us if we are to preserve and induce to activity the supernatural life of our soul. All these graces come to us through Mary. There is no need in the spiritual life which she does not understand, and for which she has not at hand its appropriate grace. She is the mistress in God's house and holds the key of His Treasury. Her Mother's heart yearns to put these treasures at our disposal if we have recourse to Her, if we act towards her as children and regard her as our mother. In her hands is the distribution of all graces without exception. From the moment that Jesus' dying words fell on her ear, Mary broods over each new-born Christian as she brooded over the new-born Christ. She gazes, with all a mother's fondness and yearning, on the regenerated soul placed in her arms by God and committed by Him to her trust and keeping. She has toiled and suffered for that soul. She has sacrificed her first-born for its welfare, she has redeemed it by her co-passion; she has undergone her Seven Dolours to give it life, and she loves and cherishes it as the fruit of her bitter pain. It is because of her spiritual maternity that the demon of heresy pursues Mary with such vindictive hatred, and seeks to undermine her strength and power as the shortest and most direct means to rob her of the life of her children, " And the dragon was angry against the woman; and went to make war with the rest of her seed who keep the Commandments of God and have the testimony of Jesus Christ."[5] Those who cling to Mary and nestle in her arms can defeat all the wiles of Satan, for " there were given to the woman two wings of a great eagle that she might fly into the desert unto her place."[6] The particular glory of Mary is based on her physical and on her spiritual maternity. By her physical maternity she commands the Omnipotence of

[5] Apoc. xii. 17.

[6] Apoc. xii. 14.

God her Son, and by her motherhood of souls she exercises the omnipotence of her intercession on behalf of men, her children.

Christ's Passion merited for Him the spiritual paternity of mankind; Mary's compassion merited for her the spiritual maternity of Christians. It is she who directs our first steps in the way of holiness; it is her influence that surrounds the beginning of our spiritual life, and her teaching and example that show us how to walk in the ways of God. She is nearer to us than we realise for though so extremely exalted, she is entirely human in nature, and in personality. She is of our own very flesh and blood. In many a trait in the Gospel can be discovered the exquisitely human and womanly nature of Mary. It can be witnessed in the haste with which she betook herself to her cousin Elizabeth, on learning the glad tidings that Elizabeth had become a mother. It can be read in her gentle reproach addressed to her Son when she discovered Him after her anxious search in the Temple; and during the course of the public life of Jesus, occurred that strikingly characteristic manifestation of Mary's devoted womanhood and exquisitely tender motherhood. We read of her solicitude to get Jesus away for a while from the absorbing work of preaching and teaching. She desires, as only a woman and a mother can desire, to minister to His wants and to give Him the rest and repose which He so badly needs. "And His Mother and His brethren came, and standing without, sent unto Him calling Him."[7] Mary has a heart that is eminently human, womanly and maternal; and all the tenderness of that heart is poured out on us, her children. She casts around our spiritual life all the care with which an earthly mother surrounds the physical life of her children. With love she watches over our spiritual growth and development, and is vigilant to check the first beginnings of those natural tendencies which impoverish and dwarf our spiritual life. She follows with anxious care the disease which our waywardness is ever causing, and constantly applies the remedies of grace until we have recovered. And when we may have fallen into mortal sin, and incurred death, she, so to say, leaves the Heart of God no peace with her tears, until she has obtained our restoration to life.

[7] Mark iii. 31.

Mary is the Mother of Mercies; her primary concern is not the administration of justice. A mother's whole attitude to her children is an attitude of love and tenderness, of a love which is proof against every trial to which it may be subjected by rebellion, ingratitude, indifference and forgetfulness. It is true that the wayward and the wicked child raises a barrier, against which that love beats in vain. Escaping from his mother's care, the child is removed from her protecting vigilance and withdrawn from her beneficent influence. But the mother suffers and waits with unwavering hope for the return of her child. The child has only to break away from the influence which he has allowed to come between his life and his mother's guardianship, and to come back, in order to experience once again the effects of a love which has known no diminution. Mary's office is not to punish or to chide. All her relations with us consist in protecting, healing, consoling; in comforting and winning pardon and forgivness for us when we have erred and displeased God, Our Father. She is all tenderness and exercises her protecting care towards us until we leave our spiritual infancy and enter into the career of trial and suffering and sanctification, which is the lot of every brother of Jesus Christ.

Mary has passed before us on the way to Calvary; she has tasted to its depths the bitterness of the cup of life. Her soul has been pierced with grief and torture in every fibre of the human heart that is sensitive to pain. All trials and sufferings which we have to encounter Mary has endured. With her growth in sanctity, her wisdom ripened. The fruit of her sanctity, of her wisdom and of her experience, Mary puts at the service of her children when they have to leave her protecting arms and stand side by side with Jesus in the moment of trial and suffering. It is then we need Mary's help more than ever. We must not rely on our own strength nor must we seek to battle with eyes fixed on God alone. We must look towards Mary. In the relations between father and son there exists a certain awe which is wholly absent from the relations between mother and child. To increase our confidence and sustain our courage in the defeats that we encounter, and in the heartwounds we receive in the spiritual combat, it is necessary for us to have that sense of ease with our heavenly Advocate, that absolute and complete childlike trust in Mary, Our Mother. We should lose heart had we not Mary to turn to when things become difficult and our temptations are bewildering. And even our successes will generate something harsh and hard, something severe and unheavenly in our spiritual character, unless there is in us this constant recourse to Mary for light and rest and refreshment. When wearied with the strife, it is necessary for us to rest ourselves in her maternal arms, and speak to her of those trials and difficulties which we meet with in spiritual ways of which she has such a profound knowledge. She has been through pain and sorrow, though she has never known defeat. We can trust her and rely on her. She is wise and patient and devoted, and, for the asking, places all the power of her intercession at our disposal. If we go with perfect confidence and sit at her feet, we shall hear wise and calm and soothing words from her lips. She is proud of her children, and like the strong mother that she is, she encourages them to face hardship and fight bravely. When our courage fails she will reanimate it. No one else, in God's Providence, can fulfil in our regard the rôle of Mary. Many would have fought well, but have suffered check and sustained wounds, finally failed through failing to turn to their Heavenly Mother in their distress and disappointment. In the crisis of discouragement that befalls us so frequently in the spiritual life we shall invariably find strength and consolation if we have recourse to Mary. She is not indifferent to our trials nor insensible to our miseries.

Furthermore she has all a mother's responsibility to protect the life of her children. Satan is her sworn enemy. The Lord has declared that an eternal enmity prevails between her and him. She is the stronger of the two and she is not inferior to him in activity and in energy. And all that energy of mediation and intercession is put forth on our behalf. An invocation to her calls it into play, and Mary, our tender Mother, hastens to succour her child who is in danger. If only we appeal to her for help as to our mother, Mary is ever ready to fight against, and crush the power of the enemies that seek to impair or destroy the life of our souls.

Jesus has given us supernatural life and He hands over to

His Mother the task of nourishing, protecting and sustaining that life. It is a strange thing that when the moment came for our Divine Adoption Jesus proclaimed it, not by naming us sons of God, but by naming us children of Mary. This is a profound mystery. It imports that it is by being a child of Mary that one is a child of God. We are all to be born of her; it is she who is to transmit to us that Divine Blood by which we are fashioned spiritually. She plays an indispensable part in our regeneration. It is true that no virtue or even holiness can produce in those heretics who deny Mary's prerogatives, the features of Christ's holiness. It is only those who enter into, and form part of that family at Nazareth over which Mary rules, that are assimilated to her first-born Son. Those who are from outside, no matter how much real goodness they may possess, are not of this family. We, like Jesus, have our private as well as our public life, our life of preparation, and our life of trial and combat for God's glory and our own sanctification. Mary plays the rôle of mother to us in each sphere. She follows our destinies with all a Mother's love and pride and sympathy, rejoicing in our successes and ever ready to comfort us in our failures. At each stage of our spiritual career Mary provides for all our needs. She is ever at our side to sustain us in our weakness, never reproaching, but ever consoling and encouraging her children, and, by her gentle motherhood, making our hearts overflow with love and confidence. And when the struggle is drawing to a close and death is coming to our release, Mary, our devoted Mother, will be at the death bed of her dying child. "Holy Mother," the Church pleads, "pray for us now, and at the hour of our death." As she stood by the Cross and watched the life she had given to Jesus ebb slowly away, so will Mary watch by us. She will see that the life we have received from her does not suffer from the attacks of Satan, who waits for the moment of physical exhaustion to deliver his final assault. No harm can come to us when she is there to soothe our last moments, and take our poor struggling soul under the shelter of her maternal love. What evil can befall us when she is there to protect us? It is certain that those who, during life, have constantly turned to Mary, as to a mother, can suffer neither fear nor danger at their last hour. It is a Mother's duty—and Mary accomplishes it perfectly—not to abandon her children in the hour of danger. Holy Mary, Mother of God, and our Mother, pray for us, sinners, now and at the hour of our death. Amen.

CHAPTER II.

SPOUSE OF THE HOLY GHOST

"Hail, full of grace" (St. Luke i. 28).

"Hail full of Grace." These simple words introduced us to the greatest event which took place in history. Beside this great event all other events and achievements—the establishment of vast and mighty empires, sweeping revolutions, the wonders of art and the triumphs of commerce are dwarfed into insignificance, nay more, are as if they were not. A drop of water may quantitively be compared to the great oceans, but nothing can be compared to the stupendous event recounted for us in the first chapter of St. Luke's gospel. "Hail full of grace." These words usher in the grandest, the only true, the only real revolution ever accomplished. The world was plunged in impenetrable darkness. In it one light shone out and that light was Mary. In that world of death Mary was the only real living thing. Mark the words, the only *real living thing* and take them in their literal sense. Upon that world wrapped in night there burst with the Angel's salutation to Mary, a mighty sun which, scattering the darkness, heralded the dawn of the day of salvation.

The extraordinary thing about this stupendous event is that it is centred round a mere girl, not yet sixteen summers, living in an obscure village, the child of humble parents and belonging to a subject nation. This humble Maid was the pivot on which this great revolution turned. The angel saluted her "full of grace," and the words filled him with awe, wonder and admiration, as he spoke them. Gabriel had been acquainted with the Light of Heaven, but here in this humble Maid he found light which was only surpassed by the light of Divinity Itself. His attitude towards her was one of respectful awe. Mary was "full of grace." We are apt to think of a vessel filled to the brim. It is a poor comparison. Grace is not a liquid, however precious. If we think of a person "full of life" we get a clearer notion of the reality.

14

By that phrase we mean that a person's whole being is vibrant with vitality. So was Mary's whole being vibrant with the Divine Life of Sanctifying Grace.

Grace is the central fact in the present order and hence the Gospel of the Incarnation begins with it—" Hail, full of grace " —" thou hast found grace with God."[1] It is the criterion by which we should judge all. A man's holiness is in proportion to the degree of Grace, of Divine Life, that he possesses. Without grace, talent, genius, ability, count for little.

Mary was filled with this Divine Life. The activities of this Divine Life are to think, to know, and to love. Mary thought, knew and loved, all in terms of God. She was inundated with this life of God. To live in this state she did not think it was necessary to retire from human society and live in an anchorhold. She lived the ordinary life of every Jewish child of her age and time. She occupied herself with her domestic duties—she dusted, swept and sat at her distaff. All her work was done carefully and assiduously. Mary did all this simply because it was God's will for her. Never once did she hesitate to consider how it was affecting her own growth in perfection. She did not occupy herself with such self-analysis. Her life was one of great simplicity. It was all directed towards God and there was nothing of self in it and that is the characteristic of true holiness. In Mary there was no self-analysis, subjectivity or undue preoccupation about her own spiritual advancement.

The angel's word must have been a great shock to her because in a unique way her thoughts were turned inward on herself. The whole tendency of her being had been outward and upward towards God, never towards self. One thing about Mary was the extraordinary clarity with which she saw God's plan of giving His Divine Life through our ordinary daily duties. She did the same things as every other Jewish maid of her age and yet, what a difference! How unlike Mary we are in our great want of simplicity. She viewed everything from God's viewpoint and that is where we often fail. It is sad to see so many good religious failing to reach maturity in the spiritual life. They are well-meaning, anxious to advance in holiness and to do

[1] St. Luke i. 28-30.

good work. All this is meritorious in God's eyes and yet there is a lack somewhere. We do not find in them the maturity of one advanced in holiness. This maturity is evident even exteriorly in the serene glance of the eye, the thoughtful expression of the brow and the general exterior bearing. Why this failure (comparative, if not total failure) in so many souls? Why this dwarfed growth? I think it comes from undue preoccupation about our perfections and imperfections. Many religious set out to perfect themselves—their goal is self-perfection and God is only a means to this goal. Much time is spent by us in self-congratulation or self-pity; bewailing our faults, or taking complacency in our advance in this virtue or that. All this time could be much more profitably spent in useful occupations. For the most of us, from the very beginning our prayer takes on the tone: "O, Almighty God, I am a wretched sinner, full of faults. Wilt thou make me perfect? Make me pure, holy and without fault." Honestly face the situation; has not this been the tendency of our prayer? Nearly always it is directed towards self-perfection. We want to be holy, to be saints, to have our stained-glass window. The stained-glass window is always at the back of our spiritual ambition. We want to be perfect angels. Our prayer seems good enough, yet we are not praying as Our Lord taught us to pray. We have not the spirit of the Our Father. Childlike simplicity is lacking in our prayer. A good child never reflects on how he is advancing in the virtue of obedience: he simply obeys. We are children of Our Father in Heaven and should behave as such. Our Blessed Lady had this simplicity of outlook. She was very mature spiritually; she rose above the distresses and entanglements of self-occupation. We shall become spiritually mature, only when we learn to imitate Mary in her childlike attitude towards God.

Mary's prayer through those sixteen years prior to the Incarnation was constant, and the tendency of that prayer was for a fuller realisation of the character of God. When the time of the Annunciation had come, Mary had achieved this realisation as perfectly as she was capable of realising it. The paternity of God was for her a great reality. She knew that she was God's child and she lived as such, and desired intensely that all men should do likewise. This was her prayer.

The Jews longed for the coming of the Messiah. They longed for the Mighty One to come and free them and subject the world by His strength and power. Mary, too, longed for His coming but she longed for willing service on the part of man. This was the way she wanted His Kingdom to come. In a certain sense, she anticipated the teaching of her Divine Son in the Our Father. Her one ambition was for His glory and her one pain was to have His designs thwarted. The Annunciation was at hand.

Unfortunately, familiarity with the story of the Annunciation causes us to lose the awful sense of wonder that should be ours as we contemplate this mystery. God sends down his Archangel Gabriel from Heaven to earth. Gabriel, one of the grandest of God's spirits is chosen to be an ambassador to a child of the earth. Look at the respect of God for this creature of His own. He treats her as one earthly sovereign would treat a princess of equal rank. He sends one of His highest subjects as an ambassador. Think of the respect of God for this child—sovereign respect for her liberty and a divine realisation of her soul's perfection. In the whole scene there is respect, love and admiration for this child of earth. God always acts thus. He is never abrupt in His dealings with souls. He is always considerate. Gabriel is chosen for this mission and he is happy. His name signifies " strength of God " or "stout warrior of God." We know of the great battle of will that once took place in heaven—a battle of such energy and vigour that before it the dreadfulness of recent world war is relatively unimportant. Gabriel must have distinguished himself in the battle; that is probably how he earned his name, and now he is rewarded by being chosen as the ambassador to this child of Nazareth.

Worthy of notice is Gabriel's lowly attitude throughout the whole scene and remember this act of abasement was merited on Mary's part. Gabriel realised that Mary was a greater one than he. There is a wonderful calmness and serenity in the whole scene. " Hail, full of grace, the Lord is with thee."[2] Never were such words uttered to woman. Yet see the reaction of Mary. Had the angel announced these reassuring words to us we would be intoxicated with joy. Not so Mary.

[2] St. Luke i. 28.

The proclamation of her sinlessness did not transport her into a rapture of joy. The Gospel narration is explicit " and Mary having heard was troubled at his saying and thought with herself what manner of salutation this should be."[3] Mary " was troubled." Why was she whose soul was the very haven of tranquillity troubled at the words of the angel?

Writers on the spiritual life explain Mary's fear in various ways. Some say she feared that her humility might suffer on account of this tremendous reassurance. This shows that such writers have an inadequate idea of the supernatural life. Humility can only suffer in those who are away from God. Mary was too intimately united with God for that. Others say she doubted the angel's origin—fearing, perhaps, that he was from Satan, even Satan himself in the guise of an angel of light. Mary had no doubt whatever of the origin of the messenger. She was far too well versed in sanctity and in the science of the supernatural not to know this spirit and what he purported to be—a messenger from the court of Heaven. You will also hear it said that Mary feared for her virginity—this is hardly true. Such a mentality implies that Mary was loving virginity for its own sake. Mary loved nothing for its own sake—she loved all in and for God. If Mary believed that chaste conjugal union was what God wanted of her she would gladly have embraced that state.

" And Mary was troubled."[4] She quivered to the very depths of her mighty soul—her strong heart quailed at the angel's words and why? Mary knew her Scriptures thoroughly. In that instant she saw with unutterable clarity all the mysteries of God's dealing with the Chosen People. She saw the meaning of the law and the prophecies. She suspected God's designs for her, and her enlightened mind grasped His mighty proposal to her. She knew a virgin should conceive and bring forth a Son, Who would be a Man of Sorrows. She saw directly what the angel's words meant and in this prevision her soul was troubled at his " manner of salutation."[5] Her fear came from a perfect understanding of his message.

All during those sixteen years Mary had led an intensely peaceful, tranquil and happy life. She realised that if she

[3] St. Luke i. 29.
[4] St. Luke i. 29.
[5] idem.

accepted God's invitation her life of serenity and calm would be at an end. This is what made her quail; this is why she was troubled. She knew only too clearly what would be involved for the person who would give birth to Our Saviour —she understood the tremendous sacrifice asked. She saw every detail, every rejection, every suffering down to the last sigh on Calvary. She knew she would have to stand by in that titanic conflict. Her vision was one drenched with blood and tears. No wonder she was troubled. She felt the mighty eagle onrush of the Divine and she hesitated, quailed and faltered as a creature must.

There is yet another aspect. We know that Mary's prayer was one of longing desire to know God more and more. Here now was the answer to that prayer. This great God of might and majesty now revealed Himself to her in an attitude of overwhelming condescension. Mary was astonished at the thought of the great God of her fathers condescending to be her own child. Mary saw all this clearly and lucidly. The angel therefore continued his message: " Fear not Mary, . . . He shall be great and shall be called the Son of the Most High . . . . and of His Kingdom there shall be no end."[6] The prevision of Mary had its tragic side but also its beautiful aspect. Gabriel said God would be born of her. She had ever longed to be a child of God and now she found that God was going to be her Child. That was the great beauty of the revelation. Thus was Mary rewarded for her life of prayer.

There was a complete change in the modality of Mary's love of God from the time she uttered her fiat. She still loves Him as her God but to this is added all the tenderness, all the emotions which accompany the love of one creature for another. Her love of God was penetrated through and through with the love of a mother for her child. Mary's thought was not one of her own greatness but of the greatness of God and of His amazing condescension. She marvelled at the tenderness, the unutterable condescension, the simplicity of God. Mary was amazed; but the simplicity of God finds an echo in her own heart. With complete obliteration of self she makes an answer in which the word " I " does not occur—" Ecce ancilla Domini."[7] To God's simplicity responds the simplicity of Mary. She is still God's handmaid; the dignity of motherhood does not destroy her essential lowliness. Mary was very truthful. Though God is deigning to be her Child, she is determined to remain in the position of His creature. No human mind could adequately express her complete self-forgetfulness. Though she was only sixteen years old she was a perfect woman. She rises splendidly to the occasion. She is undisturbed and calm in that tremendous moment. A creature instinctively shrinks from the approach of the divinity. Mary felt that dread as all the saints have felt it. The eagle-like sweep of the divinity is terrifying for any creature. Yet Mary does not lose her self-possession. She is calm, controlled, dignified. She is simply womanly. Now in this hour of tremendous choosing, she comports herself as the perfect child of God. " And Mary said: Behold the handmaid of the Lord. Be it done unto me according to thy word."[8]

True to her life of prayer, her life guided by God's tastes in every detail, she thus comported herself. She lived always as the perfect " handmaid of the Lord." The divine will was the law of her life. Such should be the life of all those consecrated to God in religion. Let us therefore, ever strive to live in the disposition of a handmaid of the Lord, in every circumstance and at every moment. Let us ask that grace through Mary's intercession and beg our heavenly mother to continue in us her perfect life of dependence and submission.

[7] St. Luke i. 38.
[8] St. Luke i. 38.

CHAPTER III.

MOTHER AND CHILD

" And entering into the house, they found the Child with Mary His Mother" (Matt. ii. 11).

It is useful to us and an aid to our spiritual progress to recognise that Mary plays, not merely an important rôle, but an absolutely essential rôle in our spiritual life. So essential is the part she plays that it is impossible for us to make any real progress in sanctity unless Mary is our Helper and our Guide; unless she is the regulator of our spiritual existence.

If I may be pardoned for alluding to a personal experience, I should like to speak of something that struck me greatly when I was recently abroad. In the schools of painting of the twelfth, thirteenth, fourteenth and fifteenth Centuries, all the great painters, without exception, took as a theme on which to exercise their art, the Mother and the Child. Not one of them was content with dealing once with the subject; each artist returns to it over and over again, as if feeling his powerlessness to exhaust its significance. It is clearly evident that their choice was not dictated by the exigencies of their art. It was governed by something higher. The fact struck my imagination and held it; what was behind it did not flash on my mind until just before my return home. I had seen a great number of pictures; I asked myself what was signified by this noteworthy fact, this perpetual recurrence of the same theme, which was yet, not the same. Painter after painter, living in an atmosphere impregnated with Christianity, aimed at expressing in his art the significance of life as understood by his generation. In every age the artist tries to flash on our senses, in the concrete, the inner form of the life that is special to his age and time. The themes chosen by the artists of any given period reveal much about that period.

These men, living in an age deeply Christian, reproduced over and over again, representations of the Mother and the

21

Child, and of the Crucifixion. It is true of course, that they dealt with other aspects of Our Lord's life, but these two themes are by far the more common. Again it is to be noted that they saw no incongruity between the two. They pass with ease, and logical sequence, from the Mother and the Child to the Mother of Sorrows and the Crucified.

The next thing that struck me, in the pictures, is the attitude of the Mother. It is a thing you cannot fail to remark, when studying the painters of those Centuries. When these artists were at work they had before them a real mother with a real child, yet in the pictures of the pre-Renaissance period we see something that at first glance might almost look like coldness, a certain aloofness in the attitude of the Mother. Her eyes are rarely fixed on the Child; her gaze seems to pass beyond Him to something or someone else. Then again, she seems to hold Him loosely; the eager clutching of the Child to herself, which is the characteristic of the ordinary human mother, is not depicted. There is an absence of any selfish absorption. She is not wrapped up in the Child, as her own: she is not wholly absorbed in that possession of hers. She does not hold the Infant as a mother holds her little son, as being exclusively her very own, *her* child of whom she will not let go. She holds Him, rather, as revealing Him to those other children who were to be hers. Her eyes, that seem to look out so far away, are regarding her possible children; that far-away reflective look in her eyes harbours the thought of her children of all ages. So does the Mother appear under the brush of the painters of the ages of Faith. What is the inner significance of all this? What profound truths are these men expressing in their art?

This is perhaps the explanation. They are showing us no individual mother with an individual child—they are placing before us one who was to be the Mother of many children, Mother of all Christians; the Mother who was to hold in her arms not this Child alone, but all who, by Him, are made children of God. Mary is the Mother of us all, prepared to hold us all in her arms. She shows us this heavenly Child Who is hers, as a symbol or type of what we must strive to be if we are to be her true children. She seems to appeal to us to be as He is, so that we may enter into relation with Him.

She holds Him out to us, not so much as her child as our Brother.

When we turn to the painters of the seventeenth and eighteenth centuries, we find a great change in their manner of depicting the Mother and Child. The supernatural has disappeared. We are shown an earthly mother and an earthly child, very beautiful often, but humanized, made individual, selfish, having lost that note of universality, of Christianity. The earlier painters had the truer instinct, the true idea.

It is by a perfectly right instinct that we address Mary as "*Mother*." A Catholic child has not to be taught to call Mary "*Mother*," as he does it instinctively, spontaneously, prompted by the Holy Spirit, present in the soul by the grace of Baptism. We must keep the term "*mother*" before us in its full significance. We must not let it become trite and conventional through habitual and constant use. It must, if we are to progress in the spiritual life, retain for us always its full significance, must mean to us all that is meant by the human term "*mother*," with the immense spiritual significance added thereto.

Mary is our Mother. Not only is she concerned about our heavenly destiny, but she is also a perfect advocate and a comforter of boundless sympathy. She is Mother as having truly and literally transmitted to us the supernatural life of our soul, as truly and literally as our earthly mother, under God, transmitted to us our physical existence. In the supernatural order we owe, under God, to Mary not only the beginnings of our life, not merely the elements of our life, but all of that life, in all its details. Every phase of it is dependent on her. No grace comes to us that is not transmitted to us through her. All grace comes to us through Mary.

She is therefore for us, in very truth, Mother of life, of that life by which we really live. This is her place in the order of God's Providence.

What is life? We are conversant with life in many forms and manifestations. What *is* life? The question would seem a simple one to answer; life should be easy to define. Yet we find it hard to convey in words what this term "*life*" means; when we try to frame our definition we find ourselves perplexed. Life is hard to define, as are all simple things.

Life is somehow identified for us with movement, with motion, with a certain type of motion, that is self-movement. Anything that moves with a motion whose source is in itself is said by us to be alive. As long as self-movement lasts, we speak of the thing as a living thing. When self-movement ceases, we say it has ceased to live.

We may then consider that the person who gives us life, gives us self-movement of a certain definite kind. What is the particular kind of self-movement that comes to us in virtue of the life given to us through Mary? We shall understand this more clearly if we consider successively the various degrees of life with which we are familiar, beginning with plant life.

We see that plants strike roots into the earth and draw therefrom substances which minister to their development. As they grow we notice how they stretch up into the air and sunlight and draw to themselves fresh nourishment. Their whole power of self-movement tends to their growth and development. Finally the plant produces seeds capable of reproducing other plants of its kind.

Then we note how little animals born into the world are capable of self-government of another kind. They react to impressions made on the senses; they move, urged by various instincts implanted in their being. Theirs is a higher form of life than that of the plant and brings with it a higher form of self-movement.

When we reach the rational life of men, we find ourselves in presence of self-movement of a still higher form. That which is characteristic of man is movement of his intellect and will. Looked at superficially, it might seem to us that self-movement of the will is but a slight kind of movement, not a forceful one. This is a mistaken idea. A moment's thought will show us of what the movement of man's will is capable. What can the movement of the human will not effect? It is a movement of the most notable force. Such movements of the will have effected transformations of circumstances, character, life. It was a movement of your will that brought you here, that led you to make the sacrifice of friends and home, clothed you in your habit and bound you to an entirely changed condition of life—one movement of your will. How strong and powerful is that movement of the will when contrasted with the movements of the body.

Is that tremendous power of the human will the power we receive from Mary? No; we receive this power from God.

We may next consider a yet higher form of activity. The angels have intellect and will. No activity of the human intellect or of the human will can give us even the faintest idea of the enormous power and vitality involved in one single act of the angelic determination, so strong, so powerful, so marvellous in its magnificence of power is this act of angelic intellect.

Is that the life which is ours through Mary? No; it is something greater even than this. To reach this life we must pass the confines of creation, we must penetrate into the Divinity itself; we must enter into the life and self-movement of God, into the power and movement which belong to His Divine Life.

The movement of God's life, infinite in strength and in power, expands itself in two ways; a movement of the intellect which in itself expresses to itself the boundless reality which is God, and begets a Word which is the Infinite Expression of all He has gathered up in that infinite glance. What must be the force of that Idea which contains the totality of the Godhead. What must be the might of that Word brought forth from the Godhead which expresses the Divinity in its totality, that Word which is truly God.

That is one movement—a movement by which the Father begets the Eternal Word. Then this Word of God stands face to face with the Father from all eternity, and out of their surge of mutual love arises a great movement, a great heart-beat of God, Itself again the totality of the Godhead. It sweeps out to embrace that Infinite Beauty, Goodness, Perfection—to clasp It, to enjoy It: this is the Spirit, the movement of Love. These two mighty surges, the surge of the Intellect and the surge of the Will, of Love, form the whole movement of the life of God. And that is the life-movement which is given to us by Mary, because through Mary God is given to us. That movement exists in us and exercises in us its own characteristic activities. It is not a movement of the senses or of the human intellect and will. It is a participation of the movement of God's Intellect and of God's Will—the

movement of God's sight of God, of God's love of God,
within our soul.

God moves towards Himself: the sole object of our life
must be God. The movement of our intellect and of our
will must follow that movement of God, because His own
Divine Life is within us. God in the soul is imparting to it
that life, that movement towards Himself. The soul in grace
is in that Divine movement. Grace catches up the soul, so
to say, in the stream of the Divine Life, that movement of
love incessantly poured forth from God and incessantly
returning to God. In that is the creature caught up and
carried back to the Centre of the Godhead. The movement,
simple in God, in creatures naturally attains a certain
diversity. That act breaks itself up, in creatures, into many
different kinds of acts.

We speak of Mary as " Mother of Fair Love, of Fear, of
Knowledge and of Holy Hope." These are so many different
streams into which those two mighty surges differentiate
themselves in the human soul.

We can say with all literal truth that Mary is the Mother
of Fair Love. She is the Mother of God; she is, too, the
Mother of that very love which human hearts by the aid of
grace return to God. We must depend on her for this divine
life as a child depends on its human mother for its physical
life; we must deliberately depend on her, looking on her as
a child looks to its mother, to obtain this life for us. If we
come to her with that childlike trust we shall receive this
divine life through her and she will foster it in us.

Mary is the Mother of Fear—not of servile fear, but of a
fear of delight, of a fear shot through and through with
trembling reverence and love. She is Mother of that fear
which is a delicate shrinking from anything that could pain
or wound the object of its love; a fear composed of reverence
and tenderness; an ardent longing to shield the object of its
love from everything that could hurt or harm it. Her holy
fear was extremely sensitive to God's honour, so that any
offence to Him was like a whip-lash striking across her own
soul. She was tremulously sensitive to the Majesty, Holiness
and Purity of God. Her fear made her surround her Child,
her Son with the utmost reverence, with the utmost delicacy

and concern, made her lavish all reverent care on everything pertaining to her Child who was God.

Mary is the Mother of Knowledge. How beautiful and precious to Mary was her knowledge of God, as it constantly grew and developed during her life. Mary was never satisfied with what she knew of Jesus. St. Thomas says that it is a characteristic of love to be dissatisfied with any merely superficial knowledge of the beloved. Love wishes ever to know more and more, to penetrate further and deeper, striving ever to make fresh discoveries, to have new revelations of the beloved object.

We ourselves know that that is true in human life. Love is insatiable; it can never have enough. It constantly buoys itself up with hope of still further knowledge, with the hope of adding ever fresh fuel to its flame; it seeks all that can feed that flame and satisfy it still more.

So it is with Mary. St. Luke tells us " Mary kept all these things, pondering them in her heart." Every manifestation of her Divine Son, every word, every act, every gesture— all were treasured up and thought over. All were " kept in her heart," pondered over, weighed, considered and used as means to penetrate further into the glorious mystery of the Incarnate God. This perpetual voyage of spiritual explora- tion was intensely happy. Everything that promised to give her a fuller and clearer knowledge of God was seized on, clasped, meditated on. This was her life of prayer; a thirsting for God; a thirsting for a clearer sight of God; a thirsting for more and ever deeper knowledge of God. She thirsted to grow in love of God; to know and love Him more to-day than yesterday, more to-morrow than to-day; she looked forward to every fresh meeting as hoping for a new revelation.

That should be our life of prayer, too. Envisaged in this Mary-like spirit what would our prayer not come to mean for us? How we would look forward to our morning hour of prayer, hoping in it to enter into a deeper possession of God, a fuller knowledge of Him, and to learn in the intimacy of prayerful union the secrets of His love.

Mary is the Mother of Holy Hope. Why of Holy Hope? It seems as if but few realise the extraordinary importance of Holy Hope in the spiritual life. This may seem a rather unimportant virtue. They consider it of less importance than the other theological virtues of Faith and Charity, and the least practical of the three in the handling of daily life. Why is this? There are few who in their daily lives act sustainedly in the virtue of Hope. We act in Faith and in a certain measure in Charity. Why is it so difficult to act in Hope?

Hope is a tending towards an object that is distant, an object not yet acquired, and possibly in itself extremely difficult of attainment. Our tending towards the object is sustained and buoyed up by the consciousness that we have at our disposal means which will help us to attain it.

What is the object, distant and difficult to attain, of the virtue of Hope? What can be more difficult of attainment to the creature than God? Only God can reach God. Is it not an extraordinary thing that a creature should aspire to such a goal, aspire to reach God, to rise to that power, that activity, which will put it in possession of God, and that even here and now? We may ask ourselves how many, when pressing on, in the ordinary activities of daily life, press on in the hope of coming thereby to God. We hope to reach him in prayer, but do we seek to find Him in our ordinary daily duties—in teaching a class, in sweeping a room, in working at the sewing machine? In these activities, do we act in the way of Hope? Do we realise that in these things we can tend continually towards God, so that there need be no moment of life, no activity, no duty, in which we are not tending towards Him. We act in Faith. We act in Charity. Why do we not act in Hope?

Mary is the Mother of Hope. Why? Mary always aspired towards God, always and in all her activities. Her hope was constant, sustained without a break. Mary was aspiring after and attaining to Him in all the minute pre-occupations of a woman's domestic life. For she did all things in view of her God—Jesus. She worked, she swept, she cooked, she tidied up for God. She "aspired" after Him, in and through all these trivial details and occupations of an everyday existence. Are there many of us who aspire so after God? We can answer that question by putting to ourselves another. What are the things that pre-occupy us? We cannot desire anything very strongly and at the same time be pre-occupied with other desires. If, at any given moment, we examine our desires we may find a multitude which are more or less strongly pulling us in various directions. Our desires are the tendencies of our life; their multiplicity is a sign that we are not moved solely by the hope of straining towards God. Mary thought nothing of importance in her life except the entering into fresh and fuller possession of God at every moment of her existence. We, too, should have that strong hope; at least we should desire it, aim at it.

Why do we fail? Why are we so often disappointed? We lack hope. We think we cannot reach God. We think that, to-day, because prayer is difficult, God is out of our reach. Perhaps we are even content with living merely on our own plane, content to occupy ourselves with the ordinary affairs of life, not using them hopefully as a means to press towards God. There should be a constant effort to realise that God is ours; that God must be ours. God has put this virtue of Hope into us for this purpose. The motive of Hope is always God, God ready to succour us in this enterprise which is the pursuit of God. When we are acting in the virtue of Hope we have not to pray God to help us. God will, in virtue of our Hope, put Himself at our disposal; He will give us all that we require to attain Him. Therefore, if we are not persuaded that by His help, we *can* reach Him, that we *can* have God, now as well as hereafter, that we can have intimacy with God, possession of God, love of God, as Mary had, let us turn to Mary, Mother of Fair Love, of Fear, of Knowledge and of Holy Hope, and ask of her to obtain for us the grace to live and act in the virtue of Hope, and thus tend constantly towards Him Who is its object.

What is the fundamental disposition for the reception of this life which Mary can give us? What are we to do in order to enter into the activities of this life? This is a very important question. The answer may surprise you. We have not to do anything except that one thing we are all so reluctant to do. The question was put many times to Our Divine Lord; He never really deigned to answer it in so many direct words. He showed that it was not so much a question of *doing*, as a question of *being;* that it is a question of being

in a certain state, in a certain disposition. Our Lord answered
by pointing out to men that they must enter into a certain
spirit, as if the being in this disposition was all that was
required.

What then is this fundamental disposition, this spirit?   It
is a disposition which brings us back to Mary our Mother.
It is the spirit of childhood.   We must be children in the
spiritual life.   A child does not have to carve out its own
destiny; a child does not have to rely on itself; a child does
not have to provide for itself.   Everything is done for it.
To be a child in the spiritual life is to depend always, in'
every action, upon God, looking to Him and to our Mother.

We all fail by being too " grown-up " with God.   We act
as adults in our dealings with God and perhaps God acts
with us accordingly.   If we are too pre-occupied about *doing*
things for God, God may let us go on and do them.   It is
not merely a question of doing things for God.   A child
does not really *do* things for its parents; rather they do things
for it.   As long as we are on this earth we are children.
Children have to be looked after by their mother.   We are
always in need of being looked after in this life.   We attain
adult age only when we enter into Eternity; then we reach,
each one in his measure, the full stature of Jesus Christ.   We
must say again, then, that it is not so much a question of
doing things for God, but of being dependent on God, or of
doing all that we do in dependence on Him.

We know how a loving child takes keen delight in thinking
it is doing something for its father or mother; the child is
pleased and the parents are pleased.   The child wants to
write; the father takes the little fingers in his and guides their
every movement.   The child is quite as happy as if he were
writing all by himself.   The father is happy, too.   The act
is perfect when done by the child and the parent.   It is the
same in the supernatural life.   To do things fully for God
is to do things with God; God helping us in each activity,
helping us to teach, to sweep, to cook, and guiding our activity
in the thousand-and-one details which fill the framework
of His Will for us.

The moment we stand apart from God, the moment we
are pleased to exercise our own powers, the result is disaster

as far as spiritual values are concerned. To human senses and reason the result may look fair enough, but supernaturally it is a hideous smudge, or a hopeless scrawl.

When Our Divine Lord came back to Capharnaum for the last time before He faced Jerusalem for the final acts of his earthly career, He spoke to His apostles. He was to launch them on their labours, on the stupendous enterprise of the conquest of the world for God. We may think of Him as a Captain with His officers ranged before Him on the eve of some tremendous campaign. What words will He speak? How will He incite them to valour? With what stirring call will He draw out all the vitality and virility, all the hardihood, courage and loyalty that is in them?

The words He utters are these: " Unless you be converted and become as little children, you shall not enter into the Kingdom of Heaven."[1]

This is the lesson of the Spiritual Childhood we find it so hard to learn. It is the grace of Christmastide. God became a Child to teach us that we must be towards Him as little children. God has given us His own Mother to teach and help us to be converted and become as little children.

[1] Matt. xviii. 3,

CHAPTER IV.

MOTHER OF JESUS AND OUR MOTHER

" And from that hour, the disciple took her to his own " (St. John xix. 27).

You cannot have failed to notice that the Church celebrates throughout the year a multitude of feasts of Our Blessed Lady. No month passes without several reminders of her glory and of her dignity. No week passes without at least one day— Saturday; particularly set aside in her honour. No day passes without her being invoked in some particular manner whether in Holy Mass, the Divine Office or the Rosary. Indeed the Church wishes us to keep constantly before our minds this most glorious creature, God's Masterpiece, " our tainted nature's solitary boast." We should strive therefore to discover some method of approach to Our Blessed Lady so that we may be the better enabled to understand her position in regard to us, and the reason why the Church insists so much on our devotion to her. One supremely consoling truth provides us with this method of approach to Mary and explains all that we want to know. It is the truth of Mary's Motherhood. Mary is a Mother. Let us dwell awhile on this fact and examine its import.

Our Blessed Lady is really a Mother. Now you all know what that word " mother " means. Every letter of that word spells loyalty, sacrifice and love. All the dearest associations of life cling to it. The word brings up a vision of her who brought us into the world, who cared for us and nourished us. It tells of days of anxious watching and loving care. A mother's love is the most perfect reflection of the love of God Himself. It is the most gentle, the most tender, the most compassionate affection on earth. A mother's heart is a divine creation. No one but God could have thought of motherhood. None but God could have given us mothers.

So wonderful a creation is motherhood that God Himself

determined to have a Mother. When He decided to send His Divine Son upon earth to save us, a Mother was chosen to minister to His needs. And Mary was this Mother. Of all mothers she is the tenderest, the most understanding, the gentlest, the most full of sympathy and compassion, the most motherly, and Mary was all this for her beloved Son. When she smiled on Him at Bethlehem her smile was a perfect mother's smile; when she clasped her Child to her heart at Nazareth it was the perfect embrace of a Mother; when she stood beneath His Cross on Calvary her sacrifice was the perfect consummation of her motherly love. The relation of a mother and son, always sacred, reaches its summit in the highest perfection that can be conceived when Mary is the Mother and Jesus is the Son. The love of a mother is unlike all other love and the crown of the love of mothers is the love of Mary the Mother of Jesus.

Mary, Mother of Jesus, holds an unique place in God's creation. By God's grace she possesses the singular privilege of divine Motherhood. She is the Mother of God. There is none beside her. When we say God is God, we have said all that can be said of God. In like manner when we say that Mary is the Mother of God we have exhausted the measure of her dignity. When that is said, all is said: it resumes and includes everything. Every honour is contained for Mary in the title of Mother of God. It is an immense prerogative for her to possess with the Heavenly Father a mutual Son.

When you think of it, was it not a tremendous privilege for Our Lady to be the Mother of Jesus! For thirty years she lived side by side with Him. She alone of all the human race enjoyed with Him for all those years that intimacy and familiarity which exist between a mother and son. During those years she exercised all the functions and fulfilled all the duties of a mother. She was the witness of His smallest actions, she piously laid up each one of His words in her heart, she knew intimately each one of the sentiments which animated Him. And to His Mother Jesus paid a perfect tribute of submission, respect and love. Never was mother so loved, never was Son so loving. Now it was in this close association with her Son that Mary learned to love mankind. It was with

Jesus that she prepared to be the Mother of Men. For, besides being the Mother of Jesus, Mary is our Mother.

It was her Divine Maternity that made Mary our Mother. When she became Mother of Jesus she became our Mother too. Her Motherhood of us is not of the body, for we have our bodies from our earthly mothers. Mary is our spiritual Mother. She is the Mother of Jesus in the flesh; she is the Mother of His members in the Spirit. Because she is the Mother of the Head, she is the Mother of all the members. The Mother of Christ is the Mother of the members of Chris because the Head and the members form but the one Christ. To give birth corporally to the Head was to give birth spiritually to the members. Motherhood consists above all in the communication of life. Mary fulfilled this function of motherhood in giving life to Jesus, Our Saviour, and in giving to us her children, the spiritual life of our souls.

There is no member of the human race of whom Mary is not the spiritual Mother, for there is no member of the human race who is not, either actually or potentially, a member of the Mystical Body of Christ, an adopted son of God, and therefore a child of Mary. But just as physical motherhood is not confined to conception and to the labours of childbearing, but must continue in the rearing and education of the child until it can fend for itself, so also the function of Mary's spiritual motherhood, in regard to men, is not merely that of conceiving and giving birth to the life of their souls. The rôle of motherhood must be prolonged until the supernatural life, which under Christ we owe to her, is beyond all the dangers that assail it. Our spiritual mother must rear her children until they have reached spiritual manhood, until they have arrived at the age of the "fullness of Christ," that is, until they have entered into the glory of heaven. During the whole of our life on this earth, according to the teaching of St. Paul, we are spiritually children, and until we have " put away the things of a child " we need the constant care of our spiritual Mother.

How greatly then are we dependent on our good Mother. How essential to our happiness is her motherly care. Our dependence on Mary is perfectly illustrated by the dependence of a child on its mother; not the child who has seen the light of day, but the little infant yet unborn. The reason for the choice of this illustration is evident. The little infant is absolutely dependent on its mother. We too, whatever may be the degree of sanctity which we have reached, are completely dependent on Mary. At each moment Mary is essential to us. We can do nothing without grace, and it is through Mary, that every grace comes to us. We cannot, therefore, at any moment, no matter how holy we may be, be without Mary's care. Her motherly care is ceaselessly active. We are the very little infants of the most holy Virgin, and our lips ought to address her as " Mamma " rather than Mother. This child-like title has nothing about it of the puerile or the affected. It shows in its own way, and perhaps in the fullest way, this incontestable truth—the fact of our littleness, of our utter dependence as infants and of Mary's preparation by God that in her ceaseless solicitude as Mother, she might answer our need.

This attitude of spiritual infancy towards our good Mother, is not a pious excess, but it expresses simply our very real condition. It clarifies and makes easier our relations with God, Our Father. Led, so to speak, by the hand of Mary, we are brought with Jesus, and in Jesus, Our Brother, to the true home of the family of the Blessed Trinity. Developing within us the spirit of Mary, a spirit that looks to humility, to joyous, loving resignation, to childlike tenderness, to holy courage in prayer, to perfect confidence, we are led to have the same childlike attitude towards Our Father in Heaven. Mary is the teacher, training us in the exercise of that baptismal gift by which the Holy Spirit enables us to say " Abba, Father."[1] Through her is revealed in human flesh the maternal tenderness of God for His children, who are in Jesus, His only Son.

We are the brethren of Jesus. He calls us His Brethren. " Go and tell My Brethren " are Our Lord's own words spoken of His disciples. He who is Mary's Son calls us His Brethren. Hence His Father is Our Father, and His Mother our Mother. Our Lord by His Brotherhood has given us a share in His Divine Sonship, and so we are the Sons of God. He has also given us a place by His side in His Mother's Heart. We are the children of Mary, for Our Brother is Mary's Child.

[1] Rom. viii. 15.

Mary is our Mother by a threefold title. Firstly, by the title of our spiritual relationship with Jesus her Divine Son, for as we have seen, Our Divine Lord has adopted us as His Brethren, made us to be His members, so that we form one Mystical Body with Him. At Nazareth, in conceiving Jesus, Mary conceived us too. By her consent to give Him corporal life, she consented to give us the life which He had come to bestow. Mary bore, though in different ways, both Jesus and His members in her maternal womb, for the members and the Head have not a separate existence.

Secondly, Mary is Our Mother by her co-operation in the great work of our Redemption by which the life of grace was truly merited for us. Mary bore Jesus without sorrow, but she bore us, her adopted children, with the greatest anguish. On Calvary she brought us forth when she offered up her Son as a sacrifice for us. Our deliverance from sin and death was accomplished only on Calvary. And it was in union with His Mother that Jesus accomplished this work. She had conceived Him as a Victim; she had brought Him up for the sacrifice, and at the supreme moment she offered Him to the Father for our salvation. At that moment her Motherhood in our regard, was completed. That is why Our Divine Lord proclaimed it by confiding John to Mary and Mary to John: " Mother, behold thy son ; son, behold thy Mother."[2] These words did not create that motherhood; they attested, confirmed, and completed it at that most solemn moment of His life, in that hour when His Mother, having become our Mother in the full sense of the word, was able to understand her maternal mission.

And thirdly, Mary is our Mother by her truly maternal solicitude; she continually intercedes for us and looks after all our necessities. During the whole course of our lives she does not cease to busy herself with us. As our Mother, Mary knows all the graces of which we stand in need; as the best of Mothers, Mary asks these graces for us; as the Mother of God, and therefore all-powerful, Mary obtains them for us. We will always be her " little children " whom she continues to bear " until Christ be formed in us." She loves us all, we who are so poor and imperfect; she loves us all with a love that

[2] John xix. 26-27.

surpasses in purity and intensity the motherly love of all the mothers of the world.

Mary is Mother of Jesus. She is our Mother too. It is our duty then to be loyal to her, to honour her, to obey her, to imitate her, to love her as Jesus loved her. It is our duty to love one another, because we are her children and she loves every one of us most dearly. It is our duty never to grieve her maternal heart by offending her in any way. It is our duty to be united with her and to make her interests our interests. But her interests are identical with those of her beloved Son. Consequently she wants us to adopt and to enter into the programme for which He came down on earth and died on the Cross. She wants us to be true and faithful members of the Catholic Church of which she is the Mother. She wants us to profess our willingness to respect God's rights over us. She wants us to signify this willingness by striving, as a united body, to mould the society in which we live in accordance with her Divine Son's programme for the order of the world. And for this end she wants us to unite ourselves with Him, through her, in that great central act of submission to the Blessed Trinity, the Holy Mass, which is the representation of Calvary. Then only can we say most truly that we are her children, and that she is our Mother. Then only can we call her with Jesus "Mother." It was from her maternal womb that we first came to the real life of our souls. Let us ask her to take us back again into her bosom at the hour of our death, to be born again, and to live for ever with Jesus as her children in heaven. "Holy Mary, Mother of God, pray for us sinners, now and at the hour of our death." Amen.

CHAPTER V.

MOTHER AND MODEL

"To me to live is Christ" (Phil. i. 21).

We are just in the middle of the Novena for the Feast of the Immaculate Conception and that circumstance invites us to dwell on the thought of Mary, our Immaculate Mother. Mary is not a mere ornament in the Christian system, something that can be done without. She plays an essential rôle in the whole Christian scheme, so essential that were she to be withdrawn from it, and were she to cease exercising her influence on the destiny of souls, the sanctification of mankind would not be wrought effectively. It is for that very reason she has been represented to us from the beginning, as a being on whom we are to fix the gaze of our souls, to have her *constantly* before our minds for our spiritual interests and imitation.

It is a truth learned by experience, that the withdrawal of our soul's gaze from her, the attempt to work out our own interior life without her, without taking her into account, is bound to result in grievous harm to us spiritually. If we leave Mary out of our lives, if we fail to address ourselves to her, not realising our absolute need of her, or her rôle in our regard we are sure to err in the handling of our spiritual destinies. Without constant and tender recourse to Mary, our spiritual Mother, our advance in holiness will be seriously retarded, and our spiritual growth impeded and thwarted. *We cannot do without the spiritual Motherhood of Mary.* Our need of her is, in practice, *absolute, essential.* It is because we do not habituate ourselves to have recourse to Mary that the difficulties and doubts, the failures and obscurities strewn on our spiritual path, tend to overwhelm us. We fail absolutely, or at least to a very great degree, to appreciate the Motherhood of Mary in our regard. It is true that as Catholics, we have been accustomed, from our earliest years, to address ourselves to Mary and to honour her by the daily recitation of the Rosary. But, may it not be, that, with the majority of us, this recital is a perfunctory devotion, accomplished as a duty, a duty that we perform in the conviction that there must be something good in it, while we fail to appreciate the spiritual significance for our souls of this prayer to Mary. For us Mary's children, the Rosary should be a most loving, prayerful turning, a most tender appeal, to our Mother, convinced that recourse to her is an absolute necessity in our lives. Do we not act as if we could pass over Mary and go straight to God? The Church is ever presenting to us for our contemplation, our study and our imitation, Mary our Mother and Model. We must go to Jesus through Mary. If we wish to walk in the footsteps of Jesus Christ, to imitate Him, we must model ourselves on Mary. We must form ourselves on her and after her. She must, if we are to be successful spiritually, play the same rôle in our lives as that which the mothers of all the great heroes of history have played in the lives of their sons. There is scarcely any great man in any department of knowledge or achievement, especially where character is concerned, who does not owe that greatness in a large measure to the formative influence of his mother on his life. It is doubtful if there can be discovered any man, who has been eminent in any sphere of life, that does not owe that eminence, in a great part to his mother. So much so, that the loss to the child of its mother is an irreparable one; and if this happens during the infancy of a child it is a loss from which the child will always suffer.

What mothers do for their children in the order of nature, Mary does precisely for the formation of every saint in the Catholic Church. They are all saints because of her. Through Mary they attained sanctity. They surrendered themselves to her, and Mary guided their steps on the way to holiness. They lived in her presence, her atmosphere; they responded to the gentle influence of her loving maternity, and, with their soul's gaze ever fixed on their spiritual Mother and their hearts filled with most tender devotion to her, they " pressed towards the mark " of sainthood. If we are not making progress in the spiritual life, if we are not advancing in holiness, let us examine ourselves on the relations which exist between us and our heavenly Mother. We shall probably find that our failure is due to a lack of appreciation and right understanding of, and an independent withdrawal of our soul's formation from the spiritual Motherhood of Mary.

How are we to model ourselves on Mary? In a multitude of ways Mary is proposed to us for our imitation. Great writers like St. Bernard and others who have written after him, inspired with his ideas, descant with pleasure on the sanctity of Mary. Her sinlessness and her dazzling purity are held up for our admiration and regard. All are extolled in glowing terms for our wonderment. Because we are a fallen, revolted race, the contemplation of Mary's sanctity can afford us a certain satisfaction. That our sinful race should have produced one creature, one human being, who has perfectly pleased God, who has been all that God wills His creature to be, can be for us a most gratifying consideration. We are cognisant that, as a race, we have deprived God of much glory, and we realise that God has received from Mary all that a creature could give.

Yet this contemplation of the holiness of Mary, this consideration of her absolute sinlessness cannot fail to help us to imitate her. Mary is really " the glory of our race and the honour of our people."[1] Our race has produced one at least who always pleased God. We take a reasonable pride in Mary and bask in the reflection of her glory. But for the practical direction of our lives, the mere contemplation of Mary's sinlessness will not produce in us an effective desire to model ourselves on her. We are sinners, full of sinfulness. Mary never knew sin of any kind. She never knew temptation in any of its forms of pride, lust, vanity, jealousy or envy, and we are daily struggling against temptation of all kinds. We are faced by the thought of our own sinfulness and of the fruits of sin in us. Day by day we have to wrestle with our own evil nature, and day by day it comes to us with an overwhelming force that we are a sinful race, born in sin, and tending towards sin more and more. The more we progress in holiness, the more we realise how sinful we are. It requires a certain amount of sanctity to be able to face our sinfulness. Were we permitted, at the outset of our spiritual career, to

[1] cf. Judith xv. 10.

realise the sinfulness that is in us, the knowledge would greatly discourage us. As the saints advanced in sanctity their realisation of their potentiality for iniquity became clearer and drew from them protestations of their own sinfulness and misery. These protestations appear to us extravagant and exaggerated, but are easily understood by those who have themselves made progress in the spiritual life. Our Lady never knew concupiscence, never had to wrestle with temptation. What can her example do for us, who must learn to resist?

Mary was sinless. Mary's life produced the flower and fruit of every virtue. Writers extol her virtues. They take them one by one, and analyse each in detail. They speak of her faith which was magnificent. " Blessed art thou that hast believed,"[a] was the proclamation of Mary's cousin, Elizabeth. They present to us the depth of her humility and the sublimity of her prayer and call on us to reproduce, in our lives, the lowliness of Mary, the prayer of Mary. But this presentation, elevating and austere, lofty and grand, of the virtues of Mary, instead of encouraging us to imitate our Mother, inclines us to keep at a distance. We realise our spiritual deformity, our lack of virtue, and the difficulty of reproducing in ourselves, even a trace of the beauty of the virtues of Mary, seems insurmountable.

But there is one aspect in which she can be an inspiration for each one of us, even the most humble of us, from the spiritual point of view. We can and we are asked to resemble her *in her Christianity* and her religion; in her devotion to Jesus Christ. All Mary's religion was made up of devotion to Jesus Christ. She was a Christian through and through, a Christian in the full realisation of the term. She embodied in herself the spirit of Christianity and we are invited by the Church to have Mary's religion, to model our Christianity on hers.

In the Old Law it was a great privilege for men to prostrate themselves before God. Men in the days of chivalry thought it a grand thing to serve the prince, to swear fealty to him. It was a great, a glorious thing to serve the prince in those times. What a marvellous privilege it is for miserable creatures such as we are to come, by the use of our own will, into the presence of God and to be sure of being admitted into that presence.

[a] St. Luke i. 45.

Have you ever in your lives sought an interview with a dignitary, some great person in the world? If you have, you will remember the expectancy with which you waited and the joy that possessed your whole being when that favour was granted. Take, for example, a person's first interview with the Pope, the approach to that great figure, the cherished recollection of that event. One greatly prizes that privilege. We like to go back on it in our mind, like to let our thoughts dwell on it. And we have the power to interview God each single day of our lives, to come into His presence, to worship and adore Him, and feel assured that it is pleasing to Him that we do that. Therefore we should value that privilege. But a greater privilege still is ours—not only can we say that we belong to God, but the New Religion makes it possible for us to say that God belongs to us. It is a complete reversal. Our Holy Church emphasises that point in the Office of Christmas:— " Puer natus est nobis, Filius datus est nobis."[3] " A Child is born to us, a Son is given to us," *because God in giving Himself to Mary has given Himself to us through her.*

Here I call your attention to a very striking fact. It is this. The great painters of the age of Christian inspiration invariably represent Mary holding her Child loosely, in spite of the recognition of the love that bound the Mother to the Child. They were never tempted to point her out as clasping the Child selfishly, hungerly, or holding Him clutchingly to her bosom. It is a remarkable trait in them. They had to paint a love greater than was ever known and in the truth of their inspiration they never painted her as clutching the Child to herself, but always as if held lightly, loosely, as if ready to place the Child in the arms of anyone who would approach, as if in readiness to make it clear that this Child should not only be hers but ours also, as if in readiness to share the privilege that was hers with any creature who aspired to have the same experience.

Her religion and ours are shown in those paintings. Our religion, like hers, can be narrowed down to a concentration of mind and heart, and imagination on that tiny Child. *To love God we have only to love that Child;* to worship God we have only to worship that Child; to be perfect we have only to

[3] Isai. ix. 6.

love and model ourselves on that Child. For her it was easy to love that Child; her Child was beautiful, winsome, flesh of her flesh, and yet though nature itself caused immense fountains of affection to surge up for that Child, her love, whilst being natural, was supernatural also, because that love of hers was given to her God as well as to Man. The union of two natures in one person had made it possible for Mary to give to her God all the love she lavished on her Child.

Religion means the love of Jesus Christ; Christianity means being like Mary towards the Divine Child. The old religion was one of fear and trembling; the new religion is *one of love and devotion to Jesus Christ.* Mary's life was one long act of love for, and devotion to her Child. Every revelation concerning Him was pondered over by her. In His infancy, in His boyhood, in His manhood, Mary's gaze was ever fixed on Jesus. She absorbed into her being and fed her mind on the thought of Him. She contemplated with emotion every change of His noble countenance. She sought to catch in these shadows which flashed across His features the movements that stirred His soul. " Mary kept all these things pondering them in her heart."[4] All she did, she did for Jesus. Her life was one of ungrudging, unstinted service. Mary never paused in her work to say: " How much must I give?" or to reflect on how well she had performed any action. She gave unflinchingly, and she gave all. There was never a moment for contemplating herself or her work, never a moment of pause in her contemplation of Him. She *worked for Him, slaved for Him,* and her life was perfect because it was a life of devotedness to Him. She never asked " How much is required of me?" Hers was a spontaneous giving, a complete donation of her whole being to His interests, in His private and in His public life. How we, in our Christianity, should be like unto Mary! We, like Mary, are called to love God. That is why our lives should centre round Jesus. That is why our life should be a life of complete obliteration of self in view of serving Him. Mary had only one thought, only one ambition and that was to promote God's cause and to serve His interests. Our ambition ought to be the same. We should think only of serving His cause, otherwise our religion is not Christianity.

4 St. Luke ii. 19.

This service is possible to all of us. Jesus Christ is not dead. He lives in the Church. In the Church, His Mystical Body, He lives and suffers and triumphs. An easy mode of self-obliteration is to lose all our self-interest and allow it to be submerged in the interests of the Mystical Body of Christ. We can palpitate in sympathy with Christ, sorrow in His trials, thirst for His glory, make His interests our interests, and thus devote ourselves, as Mary did, entirely to His service. Like Mary, we should live solely for Jesus. The trials and sorrows of His Mystical Body should become our trials and sorrows, the triumphs of that Body our triumphs. Then self-life, self-interest and self-love will disappear, and we shall live only for Jesus. Such was Mary's life and such is the true Christian life. Let us ask Mary to obtain for us the grace to live in all its fulness, in all its perfection, this Christ-centered, Christ-directed Christ-giving life, of which she, our Mother, is the perfect model.

That is the Christian life; and mark that it was spontaneous on Mary's part. That life can be lived without any great effort on our part too, provided there is one disposition—self-lessness, to recognise our own insignificance in the scheme of things, to realise that it makes little difference whether we succeed or not, that it does not matter what we suffer in our wounds or trials. We have only to think all these are of no consequence, to think of ourselves as being utterly insignifi-cant. Each of us is in a world, and in that world there is a theatre, and on the stage of that theatre there is a great actor, a superb actor, and the audience is most appreciative! And then we have this great actor in a scene with a number of lesser actors of every sort, some villains and some quite decent, but all giving opportunities to this great actor to show off, to pos-ture and pose. At times the actor falls fatally wounded, and then the sympathy of the audience is stirred: at times he triumphs gloriously and the applause is most enthusiastic. That is what militates against Christianity. We must destroy the theatre, the stage, the actor and the audience. We are always acting, always posturing, always "attitudinising," always imagining ourselves in trials and sufferings, and our sufferings are always the sufferings of a great hero. All this is selfishness, self-glorification and it is the very thing we have to get out of our lives. To do that we must realise that there is only one real stage, one actor, one drama, and that is the drama of the salvation of souls by Jesus Christ.

The drama of the redemption of souls is being worked out, act by act, on the stage of the world in which we live. It is a drama in which the True Hero is suffering an undeserved fate, is being wounded, attacked by wickedness, by impiety and by evil passion. Jesus Christ is the true protagonist battling against all the forces of evil, battling gloriously for the redemption of mankind. This is what we are to contemplate. This is the Actor Whose success must provoke our enthusiasm, Whose sorrows must call forth our sympathy, Whose destiny we are to follow with interest—such is the Christian Life. It is Mary our Mother who will teach us to live that life in its fulness.

CHAPTER VI.

CHILDREN OF GOD AND CHILDREN OF MARY

"As little children" (St. Matt. xviii. 3).

One of the ordinary accusations levelled by heretics against Catholics is that we give an undue place of honour to Our Blessed Lady in the Christian life, and that we over-estimate the importance of her value in the supernatural system. Now so far is this from the truth that it is the very opposite accusation that the majority of Christians would rightly merit, for instead of its being a fact that we over-estimate our Blessed Lady in our spiritual life, we really under-estimate her importance. As a rule, we do not give her the place in our life she merits, or assign to her the full rôle that, according to Almighty God, has devolved on her in the scheme of salvation. It might look, on superficial examination, as if all the mysteries of our salvation were bound up with the history of Our Divine Lord in His Humanity, and as if our Blessed Lady, after these mysteries had been accomplished, were brought into the system as a kind of afterthought on the part of Almighty God; but this is far from being the case. So essential is the rôle of Mary and so necessary is it in the whole economy of redemption that were Mary absent from that system or did she not fulfil the rôle assigned to her by Almighty God, the mode of our redemption would be far other than it has been. Without Mary, God, in saving man, would have adopted means far different from those He actually adopted, for through Mary, our salvation has been wrought by the life and death of the Son of God in His Sacred Humanity.

It is true that the vast majority of Christians under-estimate the necessity of having our Blessed Lady as one of the joint instruments in working out our spiritual life. If we analyse our attitude towards Mary and compare it with that of the saints in her regard, we shall find that we do not give to Mary, in our spiritual life, her divinely-appointed place. What is the attitude of the average Christian with regard to Mary? All, undoubtedly, recognise practically the force and power of her intercession; prayers innumerable are addressed to her, and all kinds of graces in the spiritual and temporal order are sought through her intercession. There is no slackness in the appeals made to her. Her intercession is invoked far more than that of all the other saints taken together. All that is true, but though Christians, by their mode of acting, recognise this power of intercession, they are prone to regard it as a power of intercession which is comparable to, while being eminently higher in degree than, the intercession of the other saints and of the angels. They consider it as being an eminent form of that prerogative of the other saints in virtue of which the saint presents before God his or her merits, pleading with them as a title to God's mercy on behalf of mankind.

Such a consideration of the mode of Mary's intercession is far from being correct. The intercession of our Blessed Lady on our behalf differs from that of the other saints, not only in degree, but also in kind. So great is the difference that no comparison is possible any more than there could be established a comparison between the life of the plant which belongs to an order all its own, and the life of the animal, which belongs to an entirely different order. So too, is there no possible comparison between the intercession of the saints and that of Our Lady. Mary pleads before Almighty God on our behalf, and her pleading possesses a power of intervention and intercession which is peculiarly her own, and cannot be participated in by any saint or angel in heaven. The very highest of the Cherubim and Seraphim is not capable of exercising, on behalf of his clients, that mode of entreaty which is characteristic of Mary's intercession. Now, this is not sufficiently dwelt on or realised, even by very good Christians. Mary is not merely more eminent in power than any saint in heaven. Her relation to God and to us is such as cannot be partaken in by any other servant of God. This is clear to us in regard to the Divine Maternity, a privilege next in order to the Hypostatic Union itself, for it is a privilege which elevates her necessarily above all the heavenly choirs and puts her on the confines of the Divinity. Mary's relations to God are unique. So, too, in God's divinely-appointed plan, Mary's position in regard to our souls, is of such a nature that she alone can occupy it.

Certain words of Our Divine Lord used on a certain occasion in His life give an insight into this relation between Mary and us while at the same time giving at least a glimpse into the grounds of this difference. One day our Blessed Lord made this remarkable statement: "Unless you be converted and become as little children, you cannot enter into the Kingdom of Heaven." Now one may read this text hundreds of times and see in it nothing more than an instruction given to the Apostles, by which they were exhorted to renounce their petty schemes and ambitions, their mistaken notions of the Kingdom of Heaven, and consent to be humble and simple in their lives. This is perfectly accurate as an interpretation of the text, but it does not exhaust its full implications.

You remember the occasion on which Our Lord said these words. The jealousy of the Apostles had been aroused by St. Peter's being singled out in an unique way in the matter of the payment of the didrachma which was due from every adult Jew. The Temple servant had come to St. Peter and asked if his Master was going to pay the tax. St. Peter replied in the affirmative. Now St. Peter should not have answered without consulting Our Divine Lord. He took too much on himself. He made a mistake, and Our Lord, very gently, but not without a touch of irony, told him so. "What is thy opinion, Simon? Do the children of Kings pay tax, or strangers?" And St. Peter answered: "Strangers." "Then the children are free," replied our Lord. St. Peter was very crestfallen, but Our Lord in order not to cause scandal, sent Peter to the sea, there to cast in a hook and take the first fish that came up. St. Peter was in his element; going, he caught a fish which was found to have a coin in its mouth. He returned in triumph. (We all notice how very different we are in exercising functions in which we are capable, alert, cocksure and so different from the gauche, awkward way we enter into the supernatural life; St. Peter was the same.) There was a stater, which was worth two didrachma, in the mouth of the fish; Our Lord then said: "Pay that for you and for Me." This incident, in which

St. Peter played such a prominent part, aroused the jealousy of the other Apostles. We find their jealousy commented on by St. John Chrysostom. Only a few days previous to this event, Peter, James and John had witnessed the Transfiguration on the Mount of Thabor. Their privilege had caused no comment, had aroused no jealousy in the hearts of those other Apostles who were not so chosen. But then there were three, whereas now in this case there is only one; and so St. John Chrysostom points out that when there were not three, but only one, there was a commotion. The Apostles were jealous of Peter and began, we may well imagine, to say among themselves: "Peter is not so well educated as John. He is hasty, impulsive, always making mistakes. So-and-so would be much better at managing business affairs." They were one and all putting forward their own qualifications, each insinuating that if he had been chosen, their choice would have been a more fitting one. Our Lord knew all that was passing in their minds and when He arrived at the house to which they were going, He sat down outside. There were children there with their mothers, probably the children of the house—little ones just able to walk. Our Lord, we are told, took one of these children and put him in the centre of the group. Notice the significance of the act. Our Lord could have reproved the Apostles on their way to the house. He could have rebuked them for their useless contention, their idle ambition, their self-assertion and their unwillingness to submit to one another. But instead He now takes a little child, a little one, not a grown-up one. The word used is "parvulus" and it means "a very little one." Jesus takes from its mother's side the little child, and says to His self-asserting Apostles: "Unless you become as this little one, you cannot enter into the Kingdom of Heaven." Now why did Our Lord do that? Why could He have not taught them this lesson abstractedly? Why? Remember that everything is clear before the mind of God. Everything is beautifully thought out and He neglects nothing. Not a single thing outside ourselves, or in ourselves, not even the tiniest crystal or blade of grass is forgotten in the eyes of God, and if God's thought reaches out to them, how much more does it envelop our life and every single detail of that life. All is planned by Almighty God, and all is beautiful in His eyes. God made the world and man saw that it was good. And when God determined to effect our redemption, and to effect that redemption in and through the human nature that was within us, when He proposed to Himself to divinise us, to raise us to a participation of His own infinite way of living, to give us a share in the magnificence of His own inner life, He would not destroy anything of what He had already given us. His power is manifested in that while divinising us, that divinisation does not destroy a single thing in our nature. Our divinisation does not imply an ignoring of our humanity, and an abandoning of what we are as children of Adam; it is meant to be an elevation, a transformation of what we are by nature. God determined that our supernatural life with all its phases, vicissitudes and necessities, should be on a perfect parallel with our natural life, so that every single aspect in our natural life should suggest something in our supernatural life; He arranged that all the natural life of a man should be a perfect analogy of the supernatural. Therefore, just as we are born in the natural, so too are we born in the supernatural order, and when Our Lord speaks of spiritual birth His words are no idle metaphor, or figure of speech. As truly as we are born of father and mother in the natural order, so too, in the supernatural order, are we spiritually brought forth unto life divine.

In this supernatural order, though we have the different stages of life—beginning, development, maturity, consummation and perfection—still as long as we remain in this world we remain in the state of childhood. It is only at death that we reach the fulness of manhood. To help us to understand the preponderating part played by the Blessed Virgin in this supernatural life of our souls, beginning with our spiritual birth, let us form a mental picture of an ideal and perfect home. In that home the child looks to its parents, but above all to its mother, for the fulfilment of all its needs. To the mother the child turns and is completely dependent on her for everything.

This ought to be the order in the home that is created for us and won for us by the Blood of Jesus Christ and into which we are born by the Blood of Jesus Christ as we emerge from the waters of Baptism. What is the consequence of this supernatural birth? In virtue of it we are dependent wholly, entirely, and completely, not accidentally and occasionally, but essentially and constantly, upon our mother. Therefore our appeals to her are not meant to be occasional, but constant as the appeals of a child utterly dependent on its mother.

Now we see a deeper reason why Our Lord took the little child and said: " Unless you be converted and become as little children, you cannot enter into the Kingdom of Heaven." He wished His contending Apostles to know, that in order to enter the Kingdom of which they had been speaking on the way, it was necessary for them to become as a little child. It was as if He said, " You have to become exactly like this little one before you can enter the Kingdom of Heaven." As the little one is in the natural life, so you must be in the supernatural life. You must be as small and as dependent in the supernatural order as this little child is in the natural order. You see it in distress run to its mother. If stirred to admiration or excitement again it runs to its mother. It suspends its whole life on its mother. So must you act. You must be " Converted and become as this little child."

In the supernatural order, to the day of our death, we must be as little children. Therefore all the aspects of our supernatural life, all graces, all needs, all wants, all misfortunes and distresses must be brought to Our Blessed Lady. We are perfectly well aware that all she gets for us has been acquired by Our Divine Lord and through His sacred Humanity. Therefore, we know that it is on God's treasure we are drawing, and that it is through Mary we have access to it.

We will never have the true spirit of Christianity unless Our Blessed Lady plays a great part or a predominating part, unless she plays the whole rôle and fulfils with regard to us all that the ideal mother does with regard to the ideal infant. She must be the channel of all our graces, the confidant of all our desires, successes and failures. Mary must rule our whole supernatural life, but just as in the natural order, the complete dependence of a child on its mother does not detract from the child's confidence in, and recognition of, a father's providing care, so in the supernatural realm, Mary's maternity does not exclude, but rather enfolds us, her little children, in the all-embracing love of God's Paternity.

Our Lord loved children, but I do not think I have ever seen a picture, in which the artist has truly caught and portrayed the love of Christ for little ones. Our Lord's attitude towards children is commonly considered to be something like the attitude of the average grown-up person attracted towards them by their grace and beauty. But even a child that was shabby and unkempt would have been as attractive to Our Divine Lord as one of the lovely little ones we see in pictures. He was not attracted by the loveliness which can be seen. When He told the Apostles to become like little children, He was not thinking of the external loveliness of the child, but of the inner spirit, childlike and dependent, which animated the soul of the little one. Children have no habits good or bad. Anyone who has advanced even one degree in virtue has more merit than a child. What attracted Our Lord to the child and why it served for Him to convey His great lesson in Christianity was the perfect objectivity in outlook and the perfect dependence in its needs of that child on another. We to our disadvantage are the opposite; we are self-centred, subjective, reflective, prone to estimate life, its attitude and circumstances in view of their action on us and our reaction to them. Our judgments and appreciations are all determined by the effects of persons and things on us. Take a simple example. If we go over in thought our impressions of persons with whom we have come in contact, we find that our views and ideas have all been noted in connection with the action of the persons on us. Those who have treated us well we estimate as being good, while we think harshly of those who give us little consideration. All our valuations are based instinctively on what we experience. In that sense we are prone to have our lives thrown back on self. What is best in the child is that it does not reflect on itself. It does not think of itself as being wise, important, influential, capable or incapable. It is entirely dependent on its mother, and that is what Our Lord tells us to be in the supernatural order. He wishes us to depend wholly and entirely on Mary; to cling to her and become completely objective. We must be as little children, never doubting, but accepting everything from Our Mother, and never asking ourselves are we good enough to get this, or bad enough to be refused it. The child does not think in this manner, but it goes to its mother, whether it has been good or bad. It seems the most natural thing that the mother should be everything to it, no matter what it is in itself. Its whole expectancy is based on its mother and not on itself. This is the lesson Our Lord wished to teach implictly when He said to His Apostles, "Unless you be converted and become as little children, you shall not enter into the Kingdom of Heaven."[1]

If we strive to acquire this attitude of dependence on Mary and cease estimating success or failure on what we can discover in ourselves, a marvellous change will be wrought in our spiritual life. This is what Our Lord wishes us to do. Let us cease to be grown-up in the spiritual life. If we can consent to be as little ones, utterly dependent on Our Heavenly Father, God, and on our Immaculate Mother Mary, then even here below, we shall enjoy the peace of that Kingdom, into which we shall one day enter, if having been converted, we become as little children—children of God and children of Mary.

[1] Matt. xviii. 3.

CHAPTER VII

MARY SINGULAR VESSEL OF DEVOTION

" Behold the Handmaid of the Lord " (St. Luke i. 38).

§ Mary—Our Model in Prayer.

Our Blessed Lady is our Model in prayer. She prayed for an increase of knowledge, understanding and love of God. The will of God permeated all her activity, and her choosings were ever made in accordance with that supreme rule of life.

Mary was an ordinary maiden of her time. During her early years she lived as every other Jewish maiden doing the ordinary household duties and endeavouring to learn more and more about God. Remember that she was Jewish. Her only means of getting to know God was the Old Testament. This gave her a knowledge of the God of might and power, the God Who rewards the good and severely punishes the evil-doer. She addressed Him as the " Lord of Hosts." She read, too, those passages which show forth the tenderness of God such as " Can a woman forget her infant, so as not to have pity on the son of her womb? And if she should, I will not forget thee, O Israel." Mary must have dwelt on these passages. Her mighty intellect, like a powerful beacon must have pierced the very infinity that separated her from the God-head and must have striven to fathom the depths of that mystery of the paternity of God. The whole burden of her prayer was for an increase in this knowledge of God. She desired it with her whole being. God is intensely real and simple. He will not grant our petitions unless we really want them. He could not act in this make-believe way. He is too much of a Realist for that. Mary really desired to know God as a Father and because of the sincerity and intensity of her desire, God granted her request. Ever bear it well in mind that Mary *grew* in knowledge and love of God. It is true that, from the first moment of her existence, she possessed Sanctifying Grace, but it also is true that after baptism, every babe is in possession of that same life. Mary developed as does every other child. Her Immaculate Conception simply meant that she was never without Sanctifying Grace. But she corresponded so perfectly in all her actions with this grace that, at sixteen years of age the angel could salute her "full of grace." Had he come the year before, Mary would not have been so ready—she would not have attained the growth and understanding necessary before she could become Mother of God. Compare with her faith and docility, Zachary's misunderstanding and obduracy at the Angel's message. Mary was always choosing what was God's choice. Religion is a *force* which is meant to mould our character to the form God wishes it to take—to be noble, high-minded, magnanimous, courteous, kind and charitable out of regard for Him. Our Lady was all that. She was so perfectly attuned to God that as it were, she drew God down from Heaven.

Most books on Our Lady are very unsatisfactory. They make her a personification of this virtue and that. Mary was a personification of nothing; she was a real human being, a real woman. Her life was dynamic, growing from day to day. Books, pictures, and whatever tends to make her statuesque are all wrong. The book on Mary has yet to be written. Books on Our Divine Lord are much more satisfactory. For a writer, it is a much less difficult task to depict the virile virtues of Our Lord than to draw the finer outlines of Mary's womanly virtues. Mary was intensely human. Remember what her humanity is; it is nothing soft or effeminate; it is always very reasonable.

One Gospel scene in particular illustrates Our Lady's humanity. Three of the Evangelists recall it for us. Our Lord was preaching to the multitudes who thronged around Him. Mary with Our Lord's cousins came seeking Jesus. She is anxious that He would come away and take a little rest and food. Here she acts as a real human Mother would act. Her first consideration was for her Child. The selfish throng was unreasonable, the people thought only of themselves and Jesus in His generosity yielded to them. Hence it was Our Lady's duty to intervene—to see that He got the necessary repose and refreshment. It is wrong to find fault with Our Lady here for calling Jesus away from His work. No, Mary, was very human, very active, and a real Mother.

Am I drawing on my imagination when I say it was Our Lady's prayer that prepared her to be the Mother of God? By no means! Always remember that I say nothing that is not backed by Scripture or the Fathers of the Church. In St. Leo's Homily for the Christmas Office we read: " *prius conciperet ménte, quam corpore.*" Mary conceived Our Lord in her mind before she conceived Him in her womb.

Let Mary's love of God be a model for us. Let us choose His will in all the activity of our lives. Prayer is not a statuesque thing. It is not expressed in sublime sentiments but in sublime conduct. We may have grand thoughts at prayer after a day of yielding to self and self-indulgence of every kind. If this is the case we are not holy. I am sure you come across dozens of pious leaflets with sublime sentiments on mysticism and on suffering. You would often find, perhaps, that these are composed by pious souls sitting at a desk with a footwarmer to their feet! No, let our prayer be a choosing of the things of God in every circumstance. Let us be faithful in our choices from morning till night and we will love God sincerely, and sooner or later the angel will be able to salute us, too, " full of grace."

§ *Mary—Our Model in Daily Life.*

Mary, as we saw in our last talk, is our Model in prayer. We saw that prayer is a petition for the tastes of God—" That we may ever relish what is right." We ask in prayer for the power to do what is pleasing to God. Our prayer is only good in so far as it helps us to do this—to live properly. In other words, unless our prayer translates itself into acts and facts, it is sterile, it is not pleasing to God. Mary was our Model in prayer because she had perfectly cultivated God's tastes. Mary is also our Model in Action.

In the life of Mary this translation of prayer into God-informed activity was perfect. Prayer overflowed into action, and in this life of perfect charity both were harmoniously blended. Mary's life was intensely active. A careful attention to the Gospel narrative proves this conclusively. You recall her visit to St. Elizabeth. There we are told that she " went with haste."[1] She did not drag her steps across the hills. When there she did not pass the day in rapturous contemplation. She did all the duties about the house and she did them well. She did them out of regard for God's will. She did not do them merely in order to advance in perfection, or because they had to be done, but because in them she saw the indication of God's will. We know that she was a good needlewoman too. She wove St. Joseph's and Our Lord's garments. We know well the scene at the Crucifixion where the soldiers considered Our Lord's garment too good to divide so they cast lots for it. Again, at the marriage feast of Cana, Mary's "womanliness" manifests itself. Her advice was asked because of her efficiency and even inventive powers where housekeeping was concerned. They knew she would be able to manage in an awkward and embarrassing situation. There was no thought of a miracle. Appeal was made to Mary simply because she was a womanly woman who is never at a loss in household affairs. Mary's upbringing was a domestic one. There is a lack in a woman who cannot cook, sew and keep house. Now-a-days you will find many girls who cannot even hold a needle.

Mary's acts were, in themselves, trivial but she did each as an act of love of God and into each act she put the fullness of her devotion to God and so received an increase of grace and prepared for a further increase in charity. She cultivated God's tastes, a habit of judging everything as she knew He would judge it. "What does God want?" not "What will so-and-so think of me if I make this decision?" was the question which directed her decisions, the guiding factor in her "choosings." She thought only of what God wanted. Mary's choice was always between the good and the better. She always selected the better and so was prepared to be made what she is—the great Queen of Heaven. It is all very simple; yet how few see the reality of it. But we find it difficult because we want to choose God and a host of other things besides, but if we try to see with a single eye as Mary did then all will be simple. Let us make our selections as she did, according to God's grace. We all know what God's tastes are—all that is noble, high-minded, honest and virtuous —all these are His tastes. Let us consider our Rule. We

[1] Isaias xlix. 15.

should always obey it with great fidelity simply because it is
God's will for us. We should never obey in routine fashion.
Every obedience on our part should be an act of *will*—a choice.
When the bell for Mass rings, each should say: " I go to Mass,
not because the bell rings, not because the others are going,
but because I select to go I will go." It should be the same
for the other exercises of the day. My visit, rosary, spiritual
reading—I do all because I want to do them. Every obedience
to Rule should be an act of will on my part. Cultivate this
useful habit. Then our every act will be an act of choice and
we will grow daily in the love of God—self must have no place
in these actions, all must be for God.

Finally, let us be persons of character. This is most important for us to whose lot it falls to make so many decisions.
A person of character is one who has strong right principles
and whose life is governed by these principles. This is
absolutely essential for us. We should have a right mind about
things—God's mind—and we should hold fast to those views
no matter what those around us do and think. We should not
be parasites. We must often sacrifice opinions for the sake of
charity but never should we sacrifice our principles—that
would be going against God. When people are difficult to
deal with we should act prudently and tactfully. When a
mere nothing is involved, above all do not be small and petty.
Learn to bear the suffering we meet with from others, circumstances and events. Many times we are up in arms in right-
eous indignation against wrong-doing but very often it is
because self is adversely affected. What worries us most is not
the wrong-doing itself, but the fact that it crosses our path—
that it touches *my* individual life. The greater issues which
affect God's plans in the world are soon forgotten simply
because they do not touch us personally just now. This is
pettish and unworthy. Let us be big; let us find God's will
everywhere—not only in our Rule but in every daily circumstance which He either wills or permits. Remember nothing
happens that He does not allow. Things will never go as we
want them to go and there will always be suffering. Let us
face very circumstance with fortitude. We should welcome
corrections; they are a remedy for pride. In prayer we should
long for, we should desire and ask for fortitude to face up to

daily situations, to make right decisions, to relish what is right —*recta sapere*. If we *really want* this favour, God will surely grant our prayer, but as I say, we must sincerely desire it. In this desire and its accomplishment Mary is our Model. She is our Model in prayer and in the application of prayer in daily life. She is our Model in doing God's will in everything—even the minutest details of our daily life. Mary, " the handmaid of the Lord " strove in all things " to do always the things that please God." Let us strive earnestly to model our daily lives on hers.

CHAPTER VIII.

MOTHER OF SORROWS.

" Thy own soul a sword shall pierce " (St. Luke ii. 35).

The day after to-morrow we are to celebrate the Feast of the Purification. In the mind of the Church, the Feast of the Purification brings to a close the liturgical cycle of Christmas. Mingled with the joy and exultation, which is a characteristic feature of the liturgy of the Feast, is to be noted a definite element of solemnity, and even of warning. For this solemn note there is a fundamental reason. Our Divine Lord was scarcely forty days old when Mary brought him to the Temple. During these forty days, Mary's life had been one of ecstatic happiness ; she had tasted undisturbed the joys of her Divine Maternity. Those weeks had been for her weeks of intoxicating bliss, during which she had feasted not only the eyes of the body on the Babe she held in her arms, but also the eyes of her soul on Him Who was her God. Our Lady's filial obedience to whatever God should command brought her that day to the steps of the Temple. After she had made her offering, and had received back her Child into her arms, all the blissful ecstasy of her Motherhood—the Motherhood of God made man—filled her enraptured soul. But suddenly, like a lightning flash striking a fair flowering tree, came the words of Simeon's prophecy which, breaking through the ecstasy of Mary's bliss, opened the door of Her Immaculate Heart to give entrance to her first great sorrow—the first of the Seven Dolours of Mary.

Before we enter into the contemplation of Mary's sorrow we shall consider why, on that day of Mary's visit to the Temple, so few recognised God and the Mother of God, and why these few did recognise them. At that time Judea and Galilee were thickly inhabited. It is therefore, likely, that many mothers with their children went that day to the Temple to make their offerings. Many saw Mary, perhaps noticed

60

her grave reserved bearing, her youthful appearance and the beauty of the Child she bore in her arms. Numbers thronged the Temple, but of the many who saw Mary and her Child, only two saw in that Child the Eternal Son of God, and in the woman who bore Him in her arms the Mother of God. One of the two was the prophetess, Anna, who had spent her life in mortifying and subduing her flesh. She had mortified body and mind, that she might be enabled to contemplate God and His Divine Message. Hers had been a life spent in fasting and prayer, a life in which the lower instincts had been tamed and subdued, a life in which by the subduing of the body, the soul had gained its freedom, a life in which all the passions had been brought into subjection. Now there is an extraordinary effect which flows from being stern to our bodies, from being hard towards our flesh, from being inexorable to our animal nature—and that is an extraordinary clarity of vision. The reward of bodily mortification is always an increased intensity of faith ; the soul acquires an instinct that can penetrate the divine, an instinct for what is God, a discrimination between what is not and what is supernatural good. A body tamed and subdued always has animating it a soul that is courageous and strong. This prophetess had spent her life dominating her flesh and the result was, that, when brought into the presence of Mary and her Child, her soul responded instinctively to the presence of God and she proclaimed that the day of the glory of Israel had come. She saw God and the Mother of God. She spoke to the " desired of nations."

There was one other whose clarity of spiritual vision enabled him, on that day, to see as Anna saw. Simeon, like Anna, had led a life of extreme mortification, of mortification which took on the form of complete detachment. He swung free of all earthly things ; not only were his passions subdued, but things of earth had no longer any hold on him. He valued earthly things as nothing. He was a man, therefore, fearless in the face of death ; for him death had no terror ; he could confront death calmly, without the quiver of an eyelid, as can all those for whom death is not a separation. Death is painful when it is a snapping of cords, a breaking of ties. But, where there is detachment, death is not painful, because it is not a separation, but a stepping forward into fulness of life. It was so with Simeon. He asked for nothing but to see God, to know God, to love God. He asked only one thing from earthly existence—God. He did not ask from earthly existence honour, power, riches, as we are wont to do. We do not ask to do without God, but we want God and other things besides. Life will not give us God and other things; it will give us God or nothing. It is the perversity of our nature, says St. Augustine, that we pray to live a little longer, instead of praying to live so as not to die; and paradoxically, our efforts to live a little longer on earth militate against our living forever in heaven. Only those to whom living a little longer means nothing never really die. Simeon was of that type. Earth had no power to minister to his lips the draught of death. Standing aloof from life, he dominated it at will; asking nothing of life, he got God, the source of life; therefore, in the end of his days he was privileged to hold Life in person in his arms, and in that hour, Simeon spoke not of death. "Now, O Lord," he cried, "Thou dost dismiss Thy servant, according to Thy word, in peace, because my eyes have seen Thy salvation. . . . and the glory of Thy people Israel." Therefore, life had begun, life was to be but a continuation of seeing the glory of Israel. "Quia viderunt oculi mei salutare tuum," "Because my eyes have seen Thy salvation"— because my eyes have seen that which changes death into life. The fruit of fearless detachment is the realisation that death is but a passage, not a change but a development, not a standing still but an advance, not an arrestation but a propulsion forward.

Simeon, having uttered these words of thrilling joy, turned to the Mother of the Child, and said to her: "This Child is set for the fall and for the resurrection of many in Israel, and for a sign which shall be contradicted. And thy own soul a sword shall pierce. . . ." Simeon prophesied that the Child would be set up for a sign—a sign which should show what is in the heart of man; a sign signifying a cleavage among men, dividing them into those who are for God and those who are against Him. For the Child this cleavage would mean the weight of hatred directed against Him, hearts antagonistic to Him; it would mean that this Child would have to bear the brunt of hate and opposition, and as a consequence, the soul of His Mother would be pierced—"And thy own soul a sword shall pierce." The fate of this Child which Mary holds in her arms is not a joyful one, but a fate which will transfix with a sword of agony, the soul of His Mother.

The words of the Scripture are always marked by sober restraint. We are always surprised at the aloofness of the Evangelists' narration of the Passion, at its amazing, impersonal detachment—a sure sign of the inspiration of God. Here we have this one phrase, " a sword shall pierce." If a sword pierces the body, it severs arteries and veins, tears nerves and fibres, causes blood to flow, but the rest of the body is untouched. But a soul is simple ; it has no parts ; therefore, the sword will leave nothing of the soul untouched. Now, why this apparent cruelty breaking in on the joys of Mary's Motherhood? One is tempted to ask why would not God let her enjoy in undisturbed bliss the joy of Motherhood for a few more days or weeks or months, or even years.

I have said that the revelation contained in Simeon's prophecy broke rudely on the joys of Mary's Motherhood. The expression is not exact. The apparently cruel words of the just and devout Simeon did not break rudely, or did not break at all upon these joys, in the sense of bringing these joys to an end. Mary's life never ceased for a moment to be a life of intoxicating joy. Mary's life was one of intense union with God, and since no soul can experience the joys of union without bewildering bliss, therefore, Mary's joys were not interrupted by Simeon's prophecy. Christian life is a joy precisely to the extent that it is a cross. Without the cross, no union; without union, no peace or happiness. Though Mary did not need purification, yet as she was destined to be the mother of Christians, God made her life as it were to consist in two streams of joy and suffering ; and if we are to be true children of God, true children of Mary, if we are to be truly Christian, our lives also must resemble hers. There is no peace, no joy, no content for any soul that is not in union with God, and without suffering, without the cross, such union cannot be attained.

From the moment that Simeon uttered his prophecy, the

sword had entered into Mary's heart. She knew that the life of her Son would be a life of pain, of suffering, of agony, of torture and of death. She passed her life in the shadow of the impending cross. We, in our lives, are sometimes called on to suffer the anguish and dread of an oncoming tide of sorrow. Let us turn to Mary. She, whose soul was pierced by the sword of sorrow, will know how to help and strengthen us. Mary, the Mother of Jesus, had to bear the cross every day of her life. Christian life is inseparable from the cross.

The great Apostle summed up the mystery of the Cross in our lives when he said: "I preach Christ and Christ crucified."[1] Without crucifixion, our souls will always remain blinded to God; we will see only the things of earth and will lack that clarity of spiritual vision which enabled Simeon and Anna to see God. The lives of these two souls were crucified lives, therefore, they saw God. Our salvation means seeing God. If we do not see God, we are not saved. Therefore, the whole of Christianity is not expressed in the formula: "Christ crucified for us." True Christians rejoice also that Christ is crucified *in* us. The sword of sorrow pierced the Heart of our Mother Mary. We, if we are to be true children of our Mother of Sorrows, must take up our cross daily and by our generous following of Him who was "set for a sign to be contradicted," come at last to the glory which awaits us with Jesus and Mary, in Heaven.

[1] Cf. I Cor. i. 23; Gal. v. 24.

CHAPTER IX.

QUEEN OF APOSTLES.

"Little children, of whom I am in labour again until Christ be formed in you" (Gal. iv. 19).

It is well from time to time and especially at the beginning of each year to consider that life is made up of a series of beginnings. It is granted to no ordinary mortal to find life a thing marked by an absolute consummation. That was given Our Divine Lord. It was given to Him to be able to look up at His Heavenly Father and say. "Father, I have glorified Thee on earth ; I have finished the work which Thou hast given Me to do". . . . Consummatum est. But for the rest of us it is not so. We are ever recommencing. Therefore it is useful for us in these periods of commencement to set before ourselves very clearly and very definitely, the purpose of our life on earth in the framework of the Vocation to which we are called.

Let us then at the beginning of this new year ask ourselves "Why am I here in the Convent?", "why have I chosen this particular state of life?" Now you are here for one purpose —a very exalted one—the same purpose for which Our Divine Lord left His home in Heaven and came on earth. You have left your homes and cloistered yourselves within the walls of this Convent to devote your powers of soul, of mind and of body to the great work of your own sanctification and the salvation of souls.

To do that work effectively there is need of great preparation, a preparation which consists in the adaptation of yourselves to the task of continuing the work Our Divine Lord came on earth to do. What a long preparation He imposed on Himself before He took up personal contact with the souls He came to transform and prepare for citizenship of Heaven! You, too, will have to prepare yourselves so that you may be able to carry out as God wishes you to carry out that same task, which is the prolongation of Our Divine Lord's own work.

The preparation for this work does not consist merely in going to a Training College and giving yourselves earnestly to studying all the courses which will procure for you a Teacher's Certificate. It does not consist in entering a hospital, spending three or four years there, and taking out your diploma in nursing, in obstetrics, and dispensary work. Nor does this preparation simply mean attendance at a University or a domestic economy school, there to take out a degree in Arts or qualify as Instructress in domestic science. All these things you are doing and have to do, and all these things are extremely important. They play a very large part in your work but a part that must be submerged and integrated in a greater and superior part.

The work of saving souls is a supernatural work, and these things I have mentioned are in themselves merely natural preparations. No matter what success you attain in these, you will never save souls if you are merely excellent teachers, devoted nurses, and well-trained instructresses. You will find, when you go to Africa, persons as well qualified as you are, putting themselves at the service of the natives through teaching and nursing. But their work has little or no relationship to the salvation of souls. So it will be with you, if your preparation is merely a natural one. *The salvation of souls is a supernatural work and can only be carried out by supernatural means.* Therefore, the great Art to which you devote yourselves and in which you are to aim at being mistresses, if you are to fulfil the purpose which God has marked out for you and achieve yourselves through the execution of that purpose, is the " Art of Arts," the Art of the Supernatural.

If you want to save souls, you will have to school yourselves to a completely supernatural spirit. This is not easy! Inevitably, through the strain and stress of tasks to which you have to give yourselves, which loom large in your consciousness, and seem important, it is easy to persuade yourself that you will be able to carry out God's work through them ; but believe me you will not! Saving souls does not merely consist in teaching them letters, even teaching them Catechism, or even baptising them. To save a soul means to Christianise a soul. Again, it is easy to have the illusion that if you save souls in danger of death and thus give them the vision of God which otherwise they would not have had, you are extending the Church as God wishes.

God's plan envisages an adult body—an adult body constantly growing. Christian people make up a Mystical Body. God sends you here first and afterwards to Africa in order to build up—" to labour," as St. Paul says for the " edification " —the building up of the Body of Christ.[1] The Body of Christ is built up through the Spirit of Christ. It is the Spirit that assimilates all the materials, forms them into itself, imbues them with life and constructs out of them the perfect organism. Therefore to save souls means to impart to them the spirit of Christ, and we cannot give that spirit unless we possess it ourselves. We cannot impart to others the Spirit of Christ unless we have first formed the Spirit of Christ in our own souls. Hence the definite work to which you have committed yourselves and to which you must devote all your energies, is the forming in yourselves of the Spirit of Christ.

Now does that mean that you are never to direct your attention or minds to the modes in which the work is to be carried out afterwards in Africa? By no means. It is an excellent thing to hear the reports of those who have already laboured in the Hospitals, Schools, Clinics and in the homes of the natives. It is good to hear all that, and to have your imagination formed to visualise, by these descriptions, the scenes in which you will later find yourselves. Such knowledge is a human aid to us. It stirs up an interest, stimulates and helps our accurate study of what we are to be engaged in. Our Divine Lord Himself, who was the great Educator did not despise such aids in the formation for the great work.

After Our Lord had been engaged for several months of His Public Life, He took His Apostles and sent them " two and two " into the different villages here and there throughout Galilee. He gave them instructions as to how they were to address the people and what ideas they were to instil into their minds. In order to prepare the hearts of their hearers for the revelation He was later to impart in all its fulness, Our Divine Lord directed His Apostles " to preach the Kingdom

[1] cf. Eph. iv. 12.

of God."[2]   The Apostles, having witnessed Christ's own methods, went and preached, and having done wonderfully well for some weeks, returned to Our Lord, extremely pleased with themselves.   They had been very successful, and like any returned Missionary, were filled with excitement and enthusiasm.   Immediately they poured out to Him their success "Lord, the devils also are subject to us in Thy name."[3] How does Our Lord answer them?   He reminds them that they have yet many a lesson to learn before achieving real success in the work of soul-transformation.   Much has yet to be done before they will be able to Christianise the world. "Rejoice in this, that your names are written in Heaven."[4] St. Mark tells us that "the Apostles coming together unto Jesus, related to Him all things that they had done and taught," and He said to them: "Come apart into the desert place and rest a little."[5]   He wished them to come apart, devote themselves to prayer, and continue yet awhile in His school.   So it is with you.   You will go into schools and hospitals.   You will have great success.   But like the Apostles you have still much to learn.

It belongs to us as members of the Body to admit freely into us the Spirit of the Head—Christ.   The vitality of any cell in the Body comes from the Head, and so it is able to function because of the vitality in the Head.   Its influence is due to its sympathy with, its psychological union with the Head.   The aim of Christ as Head is to influence each member, each organ, each cell; to impart to it His own Life, His own vitality.   That vitality is supernatural life, the life of God participated in by a human soul; and that supernatural life in all its fulness is in Christ.

To Christ was given that Supernatural Life in overflowing measure.   Into Him as into a vast reservoir was poured that life.   From that reservoir we all must draw if we are to share in that life.   What is this supernatural life?   It can be summed up as knowledge and love.   All life manifests itself by characteristic activities.   The life of plants is one of assimi-

[2] Luke ix. 2.
[3] Luke x. 17.
[4] Luke x. 20.
[5] Mark vi. 31.

lation, growth and reproduction of its species. Animal life is this vegetative life with the life of sense superadded. Supernatural life has its own characteristics or special activities. Since it is a spiritual life, it consists in functions of the Spirit, the power to know and to love. That power consists in knowing God intimately and loving Him deeply ; in knowing God as He is in Himself, and not merely as a Creator or Organiser of the Universe.

Where on this earth, are we to find a guiding image of that knowledge and love which are the characteristics of that supernatural life? I will tell you. As I was going down the avenue this evening I met a woman carrying a baby four weeks old. The child was well wrapped-up. It looked healthy, with wide-open eyes, and with a tranquil, trustful expression on its baby countenance. The relations between God and us are typified in the relations between Mother and child—relations of complete trustfulness. This is an instance of perfect confidence based on knowledge, based on nature itself. Compare the knowledge of that child of its mother with the knowledge that other people have of that woman. The knowledge of the child far surpasses in profundity, depth, insight and intuition that which any other person has of her. If we want to be great Missionaries, the knowledge of that child forms the ideal of our relations with God. It is represented more perfectly by the child of four weeks than by a child of ten years old. The child as he grows old may often become questioning, critical, aware of the faults and flaws in its mother, and so have impaired its knowledge and love which were once absolute. The knowledge and love of the tiny baby are more perfect—exactly the knowledge and love God wants us to have.

The Apostles were on one occasion disputing about shares in Our Lord's Kingdom. Our Lord asked them what they had been talking about. They were, no doubt, discussing their various qualifications for the different posts. Perhaps they could not see why St. Peter was always being put forward and even made their head. So they were afraid to tell Our Lord what had been the subject of their discussion. They were ashamed—they blushed—they held back. But Our Lord just turned to those who stood around and singled out

one of the mothers with a child of a few months old—a very
young child according to the Greek word. The Eastern
people, especially men, were not prone to think much of
children—that was left to the women. The Apostles were not
inclined to have any regard for these little ones; they thought
that such regard was beneath their dignity. We may para-
phrase Our Lord's reply to them in the following manner:
Unless you become converted and become as that little child,
you will not find any place in the Kingdom of God. You will
never occupy the position that you ambition unless you change
and become as that little child—then you will be fit for posts
of effectivity in the Kingdom of God.

My dear Sisters, if you want to become effective Missionaries, to save souls, remember that you will not succeed unless
you become converted and be as a child in the relations that
you bear to Our Divine Lord. That is the whole secret of the
Supernatural Life. We must sink ourselves and we can only
do this when we become as little children. There must be no
quarrelling with circumstances. Our hearts must be filled
with absolute faith, trust and love. Love and knowledge are
absolute in the small infant but when we grow up, they are
limited by our self-assertiveness. When we become converted
and acquire that attitude of complete surrender in simplicity
towards God the supernatural life flows into us with full tide.
We become as little children—infants of God. God does not
wish us to be precocious children. This conversion is extremely difficult. It postulates a thorough obliteration of self.
The life of a child is completely dependent on its mother for
its wants, its needs, everything—it depends for all on its
mother. So it should be with us. By grace and effort we
should reach that stage. Then there will be nothing to prove
an obstacle to the influence of Divine Life and filled with it
ourselves we can communicate it to others.

What are the most direct means in order to achieve this
conversion? You would not discover them even if you had
read every book on the shelves of your library. There is, however, one very direct way. It is the way of Mary.

This is the lesson of today's feast of the Maternity of Our
Lady. To become perfect children of God, we have to strive
to make ourselves perfect children of Mary. In the Mass

the Maternity referred to is the Maternity of Christ. But remember that is only an aspect of her Maternity. She is also the Mother of the members of Christ. Mary is the Mother of Christians. When she gave birth to the Head of the Mystical Body of Christ, she, potentially, gave birth to the members of that Body. We, too, are her children.

The physical Motherhood of Christ was only a means to her spiritual Maternity. The former is in view of the latter and therefore, in a certain sense is less than it. For according to the axiom in Scholastic philosophy when it happens that something *is* in view of something else, that something in view of which it is, is always the greater, and not subordinate. So, if we want to succeed in our evangelisation of souls, we must first study to be children of Mary. In practice this consists in a spiritual life which is based on the study of her spiritual life. In all our ways we must look to her for direction, seek her influence and depend on her to form our spiritual attitude towards Christ. Remember, Mary was the first Apostle; she was the person who first gave Christ to the world, and in giving Christ to the world consists all genuine Apostleship. She has fulfilled her apostolate most effectively, because incalculable has been the influence of Mary during the whole Christian era. Take Mary from the Christian system (God could have given us Christ without Mary), what kind would it be? It would be totally different, and what is more, it would lack that graciousness and tenderness which God wishes to characterise the relations between creature and Creator. It would have been much more austere and aloof. There would have been lacking to it the gentle radiating influence of a mother. But for Mary God would not be to us as He is. Without her, there could not be that relation of tender " *childhoodness.*"

Mary, too, had to adapt herself to this plan. Her adaptation to it was not complete at the Nativity of Christ. She had to do this all her life. She had to become a more perfect child of God. She studied Christ with the utmost attention. She studied Him assiduously. Every word and every gesture of her Child was dwelt on by her. She pondered them all in her heart ; He alone was the occupation of her imagination and of her mind. Day by day, and hour by hour, there was never a pause in the deepening of her insight into the Spirit of her Child. She became the supreme Christian of the New Testament. She did not become so at once. She had to grow by a process of thought and will which went on for thirty-three years. She knew Christ better at thirty than at twenty, and at thirty-three better than at thirty. The completeness of her instruction was achieved only at the foot of the Cross. Then only was she fully adapted for the great work that was to be hers. The work of evangelisation of the world must be done through Mary because such evangelisation means the imparting of the Christian spirit. To see how much is due to her influence in this work, you have only to contrast the spiritual attitude of even the best non-Catholic with that of the ordinary Catholic. Totally different is the blend of their spirituality. The quality of the spirituality of even the very best non-Catholic is not quite the spirituality that God desires. It is not true Christianity, for no one can be a true Christian except one who is a child of Mary.

We must put ourselves at her school and at her feet, see Jesus through her eyes, follow His movements with her loving solicitude, tend Him with her hands, and under her guidance, ponder all in our hearts in union with her. Then when the time comes for us to go on the missions, there will flow out from us that Christian spirit, that knowledge and love of Jesus Christ which has been accumulated during all these years of preparation. Mary's instruction was perfected only at the foot of the Cross. Then began her great work. She had to support the faith of the whole Church. She guided the Apostles and moulded the infant Church. Those who lent themselves to her influence, she formed to that spirit of the children of God. Such was Mary's apostolate, such also must be ours.

This is an outline of the programme to which you are to bend your energies ; to which you are to co-ordinate all your activities here or wherever you are sent. All your activities must be harmonized and supernaturalised by the vivifying principle which I have set before you in this instruction— through Mary to acquire the spirit of Christ and through her also to impart that same spirit to others.

CHAPTER X.

QUEEN OF VIRGINS.

"I will espouse thee to me in faith" (Osee ii. 20).

I am going to speak to you of a matter that has been revolving in my mind during this month of May. It is just another instance of what is a regular experience in our lives. Something which we have known, perhaps for years, suddenly comes before us under a new light; a truth which is in reality old, suddenly comes to us with a freshness and a newness which we have not associated with it before. The subject of which I am now going to speak is our vow of Chastity. What I shall say is based on two principles which experience of life proves to be principles which work out infallibly in human existence, though they are little thought of, or are considered only in the abstract. The first principle is that everything which pertains to God, everything which comes from Him or is ordained by Him, everything which has an affinity with God's Mind and Will is always positive, vital, living, with nothing of death about it. God is the God of the living, and therefore, everything related to Him must bear the stamp of life. The second principle is that when God appears to demand the surrender of something, or of ourselves, our response always has something of a parting about it. Yet, when the surrender is made in faith, it is seen that what we surrendered is returned with a higher meaning, a more perfect form, an enlarged fulfilment; and so we realise that we really have not given it up in the strict sense.

Now, by the vow of Chastity we seem to surrender what is the greatest gift God has given to man and woman in the order of nature. God is the God of the living, and that which is most attuned to God must bear on it the traces of what is most characteristic of God. Our Lord in the Gospel has intimated what that most characteristic thing is. In a dispute with the Scribes and Pharisees à propos of marriage and the

73

fate of the woman who had had seven husbands, He told them that they had no comprehension of spiritual things. God is the God of the living, not of the dead. "*Life-giving-ness*" is God's chief characteristic, and that which draws closest to God necessarily bears this impress. After man and woman, the greatest thing God created was marriage, and therefore in a very special way it bears His impress. It is the source of life; man and woman combine to give life in response to the command "increase and multiply."[1] God therefore, looks with great benignity on marriage, because it is the gateway to the world of living things. It gives Him the occasion of exercising His creative power. A human soul is needed for a new human body, and so the outpouring of life depends on the contract between man and woman. Such a contract has God's blessing because it affords Him the occasion of giving life, of creating another soul which bears the impress of the divinity. Hence marriage is a marvellous thing in God's eyes. Suppose for a moment that man and woman after they had been created by God decided not to use marriage, God's power would have been fettered. It was not God's intention that it should be so. He gave the injunction, "increase and multiply" and so He is pleased when man and woman co-operate with Him and give Him an opportunity of pouring out the infinite wealth of His life. In the Apocalypse, we read of countless multitudes of human beings, all reflecting, mirroring forth God's life, partaking of the Sonship of God, glowing with the life and beauty of Christ, and all sharing in His dignity through the Redemption. These countless multitudes owe their existence to marriage.

Hence, when we are called to the Religious life, the vow of Chastity should make us pause; we should ponder on the significance of the act and realise it fully. Unfortunately, the word "*Chastity*" does not reveal the full reality; it suggests more of what is negative than of what is positive. It comes from the Latin word which has the same root as "*to chastise*," and so has the appearance of signifying a "*crushing down*" of something. Chastity, in this sense, belongs as necessarily to the married life as to the unmarried. But Chastity for the religious should not mean merely an absence

[1] Gen. i. 22.

of sin, since even people in the world are obliged to that. The vow of Chastity is, in its full aim, immensely positive. Far from implying a giving-up to the extent of becoming atrophied, it signifies rather the sublimation of the life-giving power we have in us.

Now the strongest, the greatest and in fact the most dignified instinct in us is the instinct to transmit life. Anyone who is worth anything, or who has anything of the temper of God, will feel or should feel in himself this strong instinct not to die, but to live on and to be a power communicating life. Chastity does not mean the negation of that instinct, and when, by the vow of Chastity, we appear to renounce this power of being a father or mother—the power of parenthood, we renounce parenthood only to recapture, in a higher form, this glorious dignity. To realise the ideal aimed at by religious Chastity it is not enough to avoid sin, we must do something higher ; we must replace physical maternity or paternity by one more real, one which belongs to the supernatural order.

Hence, a life of religious Chastity implies the positive election of something that is splendid. It implies the sublimation, the transfiguration of physical maternity or paternity. God will not, so to say, have us elect to become atrophied. We are all expected to leave life after us, and we have not fulfilled our purpose in life unless we do so. Every virgin is, in a real sense, bound to be a mother. If she is not a mother she is, in a sense, not truly a virgin. This is but another of the great paradoxes of our religion on which we dwell but too little. We in religion, both men and women, are not living the full virginal life unless we are *spiritual* fathers and mothers; we are not meant to be sterile human beings. We must, therefore, in order to live up to the demands of our sacred state, bend all our energies on the achievement of this spiritual parenthood. Where shall we learn to realise this obligation? We shall learn it from Mary, whose radiant purity surpassed that of all other creatures—for she is Virgin of Virgins. We shall learn it from Mary, who, being Mother of God, is also a source of life for every child of Adam—for she is Mother of men.

Let us consider, for a moment, what God had planned

when He created our first parents. He had intended that
every child would come into this world a child of grace. Eve
was to be the transmitter of life, both natural and supernatural, to all her children. She would, so to speak, be mul-
tiplied as time went on, according as every woman would
share with her the task of transmitting what she had received.
Thus, in God's plan, every being was to look to woman as
the source of everything of dignity and worth. But God's
plan was frustrated, defeated. Yet, as always, He used the
defeat to triumph in a more marvellous way. And so, we
can expect to find, in the restored order, the original plan
which He had in mind, but in a more splendid and more
glorious form.

God has given to the world Mary Immaculate, Virgin
Mother of His Son, to be the source and fount of life to all
men. Mary was constituted, under Christ, the Mistress of
the whole human race. In God's plan, all are to enter into life
through her. In this plan too, every woman must co-operate
with Mary, must share in the rôle of Mary, just as she would
have shared, in God's original plan, in the rôle of Eve. Even
now, every woman is to be a source of life, sharing with others
what she has received. The Christian mother is meant to
give physical life to her child, but she is meant to give it
more than just that. She must give it the complete human
life, which is a combination of the natural and the supernatural. But this task is not committed to the married woman
alone. Every woman, whatever her sphere of work, is meant
to be a transmitter, a source of supernatural life to all with
whom she comes in contact, and in order to transmit it, she
must first possess it. Of every woman in the Christian scheme,
there is demanded instinctively the highest virtue and the
highest ideal in the supernatural order. No woman may live
for herself alone ; women must beget, if not in the body, then
in the spirit. She must be, if she is called to the state of
Virginity, a spiritual mother, and she cannot be a spiritual
mother unless she moulds herself on the Virginity and the
Maternity of Mary. She must, like Mary, consecrate all
there is of woman in her to God. This means more than just
a renouncement of marriage ; it means that all her tendencies,

all her movements of affection and self-sacrifice, all her devotedness and care be directed Godwards.

"And Mary said to the angel: How shall this be done,
because I know not man? And the angel answering, said to
her: The Holy Ghost shall come upon thee and the power
of the Most High shall overshadow thee. And therefore also
the Holy which shall be born of thee shall be called the Son
of God. . . . And Mary said: Behold the handmaid of the
Lord: be it done to me according to thy word."[2] Can we
imagine anything more tremendous, anything more fraught
with far-reaching consequences than the scene here described
by St. Luke? And when the prince of the heavenly court
withdrew in hushed respect and wondering admiration from
Mary's presence, he left her, not only Queen of Virgins, but
also Mother of God. By her virginity, by her immaculate
purity God had made her worthy to be His Mother, and being
Mother of God, she thereby was constituted the source of
life for all those who would be redeemed by Him.

If we represent redeemed humanity as a great pyramid at
whose apex stands Our Blessed Lady, we shall be enabled to
realise the importance of her rôle in the work of the
Redemption. Lines radiating from the apex of that great
pyramid represent the streams of life which flow to humanity
from her. Not a drop of life comes to us but through her.
That is why, in the Christian scheme, Mary is the ideal and
model for every woman. The shadow of Our Blessed Lady
falls over every woman true to her womanhood. That is
the true dignity of woman. It is a strange thing that woman
can look her dignity in the face and refuse to accept it. In
the world of to-day, this is one of the most fertile sources of
disintegration—woman refusing to take the place she is meant
to hold.

Now, when a young woman makes a vow of Chastity her
profession implies the will to rise to a position which is model-
led on that of the Virgin Mother, at the apex of the pyramid of
humanity, transmitting life. In order to realise this, she must
have, in the order of grace, what corresponds to the power
of fecundity in the order of nature. She must develop, by

[2] Luke i. 34-38.

mind and will, this power of spiritual fecundity, this power to live on. She must train herself to be a spiritual mother.

Listen very carefully to this. Comparatively few religious have a full understanding of their vocation. A woman who enters the religious state, cannot, in a sense, be what she should be, unless she realises that every human being is potentially her child. It is her duty to impress a certain form on everyone with whom she comes in contact. Too often she does the opposite ; she uses her powers to draw others to herself. She is never meant to attract to herself. She is meant to give, to give always, and in order to give she must first possess. Her first concern should be to possess in herself a fullness of the life of God. She must *desire* to possess it ever more and more. She must mould herself on Mary.

In Mary there was a tremendous power of giving, of self-sacrifice. She did not seek to draw others to herself. And so, if you are self-seeking, you will ruin yourself and others. Like Eve, you will become a source of perdition. Self must be eliminated from your life ; you must train yourself to be generous, to give to everybody, to give impartially, to rise superior to your own petty preferences. If you are to be a spiritual mother, then you must be *self-sacrificing*.

A second, and indeed a most important quality which you must learn from Our Lady is *Modesty*. Modesty is not to be understood in a small, petty way. The word comes from the Latin for "*measure*," and signifies restraint. There must be restraint in all your ways, in your deportment, your language, your bearing. There should be poise, balance, order, in all that concerns your dealings with others. Begin with the restraint of your curosity. Learn to see only what you are meant to see ; withdraw your gaze from everything except from what it is useful and important for you to see. This will entail constant mortification. Seek to see only what is beautiful and good, what draws to God. Train yourself to look only at what uplifts. Modesty in the sense of touch is practised in the control of the hands. Teach your hands to serve only to usefulness, to beneficence, to charity, and never use them for self-satisfaction.

Another quality you can learn from Mary is *dignity*. Its name is derived from the word which signifies "worth," and so implies the sense of one's own value. Attend carefully to this. Every woman, by the mere possession of womanhood, possesses something of immense sacredness and worth. Therefore, dignity for you means the recognition of that worth and the resolve to preserve that womanhood as one would preserve a precious jewel. You must, yourself, regard it with reverence and demand reverence for it from others, both men and women. Womanhood is something sacred, because of the rôle God has given to woman in His plan.

Chesterton says that it is unpardonable in a woman to be undignified, and unpardonable in a man to be dignified: as usual he expresses a profound truth. For us men, there is the battle of life with its stress and its asperities. Woman is the guardian of the sanctities of life, and so dignity is especially demanded in her. The spirit of modern life is to attack everything that contributes to that dignity. In the world in which we live, fashions, games, dress, everything, would seem to have as aim the destruction of this dignity, the rejection of which, spells the complete degradation of womanhood.

To realise motherhood, then, you must be like Mary in all things. Like her you must be devoted to Jesus. You must foster Him, cherish Him, devote yourself entirely to His interests, giving birth to Him in your own soul, and in the souls of others. Every woman, by being what she is meant to be wields an immense power for good. In the ordinary duties of the day goodness should radiate from her and impress the souls with whom she comes in contact.

There is a wonderful co-operation between God the Holy Ghost and Our Blessed Lady. Mary chose virginity and received as reward God the Holy Ghost, who is Love personified as her Spouse. God's personified Love formed the Sacred Humanity of God the Son in her virginal womb, and made her the Mother of mankind. You also have received the Holy Ghost. He dwells in your souls, and your bodies are His temples. He is dwelling in you, to reproduce on a smaller scale, but in a very real way, the purpose He achieved in Mary. He is espoused to you, as He was to her, with the object of forming Christ in you, and giving Him to others through you. His first work is to mould your souls to that of

Mary. In the soul of woman, the work of the Holy Ghost is to form her soul to the spirit of Mary, to the fostering of the life of God in herself and in others. To be like Mary, then, must be the trend and the object of all your desires. The Holy Ghost is in your souls, not simply as an ornament, but also to *work;* and He will respond only when asked. Your appeal must be that He will mould you to the form of Mary. For this work, as in the case of Mary, there is postulated an intense ardour, an intense love of God. Love is the source of fecundity, and through the action of the Holy Ghost in your souls you will become fertile and fruitful in good.

This, then, must be your devotion to Our Blessed Lady; not a petty, trivial devotion, but a devotion that goes down to the root of reality. Be as great as God has made you. You are called to be like Mary, and you cannot be like Mary unless you renounce your own interests, your own small concerns, for those of Jesus. Mary is the supreme and perfect woman. She is both Virgin and Mother, and her maternity draws its boundless fecundity from her virginity. She appeared to renounce marriage, but it was only to get it back in a glorified form, being espoused to, and made fruitful by, the Holy Ghost. She appeared to renounce a family, and yet all ages proclaim her Mother. Mary is the mother of the living, of all mankind, and so has a boundless family. She gave up supremely, and she got back supremely. She receives the hundredfold for what she seemed to renounce. She appeared to give up the power of transmitting life, and instead, she became the source of life for every child of Adam.

That, then, is the meaning of your life of Chastity, and that is what it leads to. You do not give up motherhood; you have it sublimated. You renounce it only to receive it back in a more perfect and more glorious form. God never takes anything from us except to give it back a hundredfold. Your life must be, in a very real way, a prolongation of the life of Mary. " I beseech you, therefore, to walk worthy of the vocation in which you are called."[3]

³ Eph. iv. 1.

CHAPTER XI.

QUEEN OF THE MOST HOLY ROSARY.

"Mary kept all these words pondering them in her heart" (Luke ii. 19).

Today being the Feast of the Most Holy Rosary, it is only fitting that we give a few moments to the consideration of the value of the Rosary as an expression of our Faith, and as an expression of what we can see ever more clearly as one of the most difficult, though one of the most consoling truths of our religion—the extremely intimate and mysterious part played by Our Lady in the work of Redemption.

Since our infancy, we have been taught the important rôle played by Our Lady, and have learned it with a kind of hereditary instinct. Yet it is strange how truths, with which we have been long familiar, take on a new and deeper significance in the light of a sudden illumination—a flash on our minds, scattering the darkness and revealing things in their true perspective. It is like what we experience in a tropical storm, the intense darkness is suddenly lit up by a vivid and intense lightning flash, making trees and even the very leaves on them stand out with a new distinctness. So in our lives truths which we may have known for years suddenly appear as having been hitherto as darkness compared with the light in which we suddenly see them. We are made aware especially of the harmony of each detail with the others. Everything is now in its true perspective.

It seems to me that the crowning grace of faith and of the spiritual life is such a realisation of the immense import of the work of Our Blessed Lady in our Redemption. The intense antagonism of heresy to this truth should make us suspect that. Protestantism is a strange spirit. It is still stranger how many, especially in England and Germany, who have had and still have such an intense devotion to the Old and

81

New Testament can read " all nations shall call me blessed "[1] in St. Luke's Gospel, and yet in face of all that, be amazingly eager to brush aside Our Blessed Lady and give her no part in the work of Our Redemption. Their attitude is extraordinary in every way—they hold that she detracts from the Mediator the honour which is His due. This only illustrates the falsity of their attitude of mind, since it is in direct conflict with Sacred Scripture. Such a mentality illustrates the instinct of heresy which is really the instinct of the devil, and so points to the far-reaching importance of what is attacked, because the object of attack must have a significance which we Catholics do not understand or realise. It is not God's fault that the dogma is obscure for us. And sad it is to admit that for some it seems obscure.

For God this rôle of Our Lady is of vast significance. Let us go back to the origin of things ; when God said to our First Parents that He would not allow the work of Satan to triumph, it is strange that at that moment He should speak not only of His Son, but of the Woman. " I will put enmities between thee and the woman, between her seed and thy seed."[2] It is extraordinary how the whole drama of humanity should turn on the conflict between the Woman and Satan. God said: " She shall crush thy head and thou shalt lie in wait for her heel."[2] It would thus seem that all depended on her, and that the conflict lay entirely between Satan and the Woman. We do not realise this and perhaps will not until after our death. The saints did, but we cannot conceive how important her rôle is, or how influential is her action. God sees it ; the devil sees it, but we only dimly. Again when Isaias uttered his great prophecy of the Incarnation, the main stress is on the " *Rod* " and the " *Root of Jesse* "—Our Blessed Lady, and not on the " *Flower*,"—Our Lord Himself —which was to blossom on that Rod.

Now we come to the Rosary. You will excuse the element of autobiography in what I am going to say, as it will illustrate the truth I wish to stress. When I was a small boy the May devotions were very impressive, and left an extraordinary impression on the minds of children. The devotions

[1] St. Luke i. 48.

[2] Gen. iii. 15.

were very well attended. The people gathered before a picture of Our Lady of Perpetual Succour with candles lighting around it, where they recited the Rosary with the priest. Somehow Our Lady was made very essential, very central, as the attention of the whole congregation was drawn to her. All seemed to converge on her for the time, rather than on the main Altar where the Blessed Sacrament was reserved. There was a strange appeal in the reiteration of the invocations, a potency and mystery, a sense of the confidence of children, as if the whole world was lifted to the supernatural, where sweetness replaced all the hardness, coldness and hurts of this life. These May evenings re-created something real, and placed us in a realm where all the hardness and bitterness were removed, and an air of other-worldliness and unearthly sweetness remained. Before I went to school, I remember wondering when the priest gave out the Rosary and named the Joyful, Sorrowful and Glorious Mysteries, why he should speak of something not relating to the Hail Mary which we were reciting. I wondered what could be the reason and the connection between these events in Our Lord's life and the Rosary. I could never see why we should introduce these other things when talking to the Blessed Virgin. My child-mind could not solve it, and it has taken long years to realise that the connection is essential, not merely accidental; that it is not a haphazard way invented by the Church to help us to say the Rosary without distractions. It is nothing so artificial as that; the Church was guided by the Holy Ghost in so planning the Rosary.

The whole Christian dogma demands that all the mysteries of salvation should revolve around Our Lady in a way we cannot fully understand. Human reason judges otherwise. Typical of this is the Protestant mind which maintains that they should revolve around the Person of Our Lord. That would seem to us the more perfect way, but God sees otherwise. Someone has spoken of the humility of God—a very daring expression. But there is a profound truth in it, as it seems that in all the work of God, He strives to efface Himself and uses a human person as His medium—Our Lady—who is human through and through, one completely of this earth—human in everything. God in His extraordinary con-

descension makes the whole series of mysteries revolve around
the person of Our Blessed Lady like so many orbs and planets
round their centre. Always the mysteries seem to revolve
around the Blessed Virgin as if she, not her Son, had the
central rôle. This, however, does not take place in a way that
effaces Our Lord, but in one which harmonises completely
with the truth that Our Lord is Mediator.

Beginning with the Annunciation, we get the first insight
into Mary's rôle of mediation. Our Lady's purity, her holiness of soul, and above all her *faith* started the whole revolution of the mysteries and established the harmony between
them. We admire her faith especially, because remember,
she was invited to take up a unique position when she was
asked to become the Mother of God. Faith is the pivot of
all the mysteries and because she believed, Our Lady is put
at the forefront in the Annunciation.

In the *Visitation*, the second mystery, we see her already as
the *instrument of salvation and sanctification*. She went with
haste into the hill country of Judea, and the effect of her
coming to the house of Elizabeth shows her as literally the
bearer of salvation. The soul of John was filled with the
Holy Ghost and the very sound of her voice generated prophecy so that Elizabeth uttered these memorable words:
" Blessed art thou among women," thereby revealing the
immense potency of this young virgin.

Again in the *Nativity* we reflect on the fact that the Sacred
Humanity of Jesus was formed from her own flesh and blood,
so that It is part of herself as every child is of its mother.
This fact again shows us how she has brought salvation into
the world. That humanity has been taken from her is a
reversal of the original order. Eve has been taken from Adam.
God has followed a policy of reverse in the second economy
according to the theologians. Salvation now comes from the
woman while woman came from man in the former plan.

In the *Presentation* Our Lady comes to present the
Victim in the Temple ; *she comes to offer the Victim*
which will rescue the human race from the power of Satan.
She comes of her own bidding ; and lest the reason of His
coming might be obscure, Simeon, who had come by the
Spirit into the Temple, is there to explain and let us see that

she was making a sacrifice in allowing the sword to be plunged into her soul and in surrendering Her Divine Son for the salvation of mankind. She seemed to be ransoming Him with the doves; in reality, she was offering Him for the sacrifice of thirty-three years later, for in that sacrifice Mary was co-offerer with Christ.

The Finding in the Temple is a most wonderful mystery which we can never really fathom; it is, in truth, one of the most interesting of the whole series. There is a possible symbolism in the loss and finding. Mankind through its own fault had lost God for many ages, and now after groping for centuries, finds Him at last through Mary. *She finds Him for us;* through her we have recovered God in the full meaning of the French word, "recouvrer," which implies more than our English word "recover."

In *the three Sorrowful Mysteries,* the Agony, the Scourging and the Crowning with Thorns—there is no mention of Our Blessed Lady, and yet we have the instinctive belief that *in spirit she saw all and accepted all long before.* We do not need the revelations of the saints to tell us all that. What a piteous picture she presents to our contemplation! She was associated with all these sorrowful scenes, but not allowed to indulge in her sorrow, but to *will* it; her part was not to protest but to accept—to fulfil all she had promised in the Temple—" Thine own soul a sword shall pierce."[3] The word " pierce " in the Scripture contains no exaggeration but is of fearful accuracy. The spirit is simple, and so there is no place untouched—all is pierced, torn and rent. Her Immaculate Heart was transfixed.

In *the Carrying of the Cross and the Crucifixion,* Our Lord brings her in to show us in a vivid and dramatic way her rôle. She cannot turn away her eyes or veil her face from the terrible sight. It is hard to look on one who is dear to us plunged in suffering. Yet Mary had to do all this. At the Crucifixion—the consummation—she is co-sufferer with the God-man; in union with Him she wills our salvation; she wills the sacrifice of her Son, not merely by accepting it but by positively willing it. She loved mankind so much that she willed to surrender Our Lord to the tortures of Calvary

[3] St. Luke ii. 35.

for men. It was no mere acceptance ; but *she was there as co-offerer and co-redemptrix*. Again the whole plan of the Passion shows her protagonistic rôle all through.

In the *Glorious Mysteries* this is even more fully shown. Our Lord appeared to her first. Why? Because her faith alone survived these three days ; she was the Ark of salvation because in her alone—not even in the Apostles, as we know —the spark of faith survived during the three days. Mary's faith is the explanation of the Rosary's singular efficacy in preserving the faith among Christians especially in times of trial and persecution.

In the *Ascension and Decent of the Holy Ghost*, there is also pointed reference to Our Lady's presence . she was in the midst of the Apostles. How different from our human views. Suppose we had to plan things, we would have arranged that she go to Heaven with Our Lord at the Ascension. His work was done on earth, but not hers. He lives on in His Mystical Body and so Our Lady must be there to foster the Mystical Christ. This is the reason why Our Blessed Lady had to remain all those long years—fifteen according to tradition—on earth after the Ascension of Our Lord. All that time, she was a true mother to the Infant Church—the Mystic Christ ; her counsels, her faith, her revelation of the mysteries which she had kept and pondered in her heart, the potency of her prayers, prepared the Apostles for the descent of the Holy Ghost and for their subsequent work.

The *Assumption* and *the Crowning* are peculiarly her own. In the latter we see God crowning her as if she had been the Author of salvation, which in a sense is true, for was she not co-offerer in her Son's sacrifice? She had to surrender Christ —to sacrifice Him, " for us men and our salvation." She had shared in the whole scheme of Redemption by the suffering in every fibre of her soul. And now in Heaven, she is crowned with glory—a fitting reward for her life of love and sacrifice.

All this is revolting to the Protestant mind, and we also shrink somewhat from it because we are tainted with Protestantism. We tend to look on hers as a mere mechanical rôle. But Our Lady's agency has been an immensely positive one. She was not a mere passive instrument, but she played, in the work of Redemption, a very definite part, which God wishes us to understand.

The Rosary is a compendium of our faith, the faith of Catholics, not of Protestants. In it we have everything, not in abstract terms, but in the concrete form of the mysteries as portrayed with the emotions and feelings of a woman's soul. We begin the Rosary with the Creed—a compendium of all the mysteries of our faith down to the Four Last Things. The Our Father establishes the relation of father and son between us and God. The mysteries follow as the consequence of that, and in the " Hail Mary " we have a glorification of Mary for starting the whole train of these mysteries. Like children who delight in the reiteration of what they find satisfactory, we never tire of the repetition of this chant of her greatness.

Children are a very interesting study, and a study which sheds great light on our religion. While they delight in having a thing repeated again and again, the adult seeks reality in change. Spirituality finds reality in what is abiding; not in what is continuously changing. For spirituality, the abiding reality never changes but ever presents new facets. It is ever new and yet strangely old. We see the symbolism of this in the attitude of the child as expressed in the characteristic phrase: " Do it again."

The Rosary is the prayer of the child repeating over and over again the intensely satisfying fact that a human person found favour with God. " Hail Mary, full of grace, the Lord is with thee."[4] This is the reality of all time, and we charm ourselves and Our Lady by repeating over and over again that she has won favour with God, that she is the cause of all our weal, all our happiness. It is an inexhaustible wonder, how we owe all to her.

Then the " Holy Mary, Mother of God, pray for us sinners " expresses her power of intercession. " We are not like you. . . Pray for us, *now* and at the hour of our death."

Tertullian says very beautifully somewhere, that when we are praying together we are like a group of children catching hands and surrounding a father to ask for something. In the Rosary—a " corona "—we surround Our Blessed Lady as children and coax her ; it is a coaxing prayer, calling to her

[4] Luke i. 28.

mind all that was hers, the glories and benefits bestowed on her, so that she may give us all we desire. We constrain her by our reiteration. The Rationalists cannot understand this, they have a supreme scorn for such reiteration. . . . But that is the child's way and the way God meant for us. This is the Way of the Rosary.

CHAPTER XII.

THE TRUE GREATNESS OF MARY.

" Yea, rather blessed are they who hear the word of God and keep it "
(St. Luke xi. 28).

The whole Christian world owes an immense debt of gratitude to St. Francis of Assisi because of the idea born of his genius which issued in the structure of the first Christmas Crib. The Crib brings vividly before our imagination a representation of that great mystery of love—the Incarnation. All down the ages men have striven to perfect the work of St. Francis. Children are impressed by this concrete representation as no other lession could impress them. As we gaze on these images—usually of no great artistic value— we see the animals, the shepherds and St. Joseph, but especially do our eyes wander from the Child to His Mother and from the Mother to her Child. We are filled with the thought of Mary's greatness. He was her Child, and yet He was the God of heaven and earth. Even here there is a danger for us—a danger of gliding into false values, and a corrective becomes necessary. It is a corrective that God found necessary to apply on at least two occasions during His public ministry. He found it necessary to put things into their proper order of worth.

We remember the incident when Our Divine Lord was preaching to the crowd, and a woman cried out in wonder and admiration, " Blessed is the womb that bore Thee."[1] She praised His Blessed Mother. Our Lord paused in His discourse. His thoughts may have wandered back to Bethlehem, and the first night He was ever held in Mary's arms. He too, saw Mary's greatness. But He knew where her real greatness lay. The words of the woman who had just spoken suggested that Mary's greatness rested in the mere fact of the divine Maternity ; but this is not fully the truth. The divine

[1] Luke xi. 27.

89

Maternity was a glorious privilege; it was, as it were, the *root* of Mary's greatness. Nevertheless, if we consider the divine Maternity merely in itself and *apart from* the graces with which Mary was adorned in view of it—considered in that isolated way, it did not constitute the true greatness of Mary. That true greatness lay rather in the sanctifying Grace which she possessed, in an altogether outstanding degree, within her soul. Mary, with the help of God's grace, and by her own free co-operation, had heard the word of God, and kept it. She could be addressed by an angel as " Full of Grace."[2] Therein lay her greatness. Our Divine Lord would have us realise the true greatness of His Mother, and so, to the woman who had spoken, He answered: " Yea rather, blessed are they who hear the word of God and keep it."[3]

On another occasion, when Mary sought to draw Jesus away from the multitudes, so that He might take a little food and rest, His eyes wandered over the crowd of listeners, and He said: " Who is My Mother? . . . . Whoever shall do the will of My Father who is in heaven, he is My brother and sister and mother."[4] Our Lord insisted on that point.

Mary was undoubtedly great but He would insist that she was so because of the love she bore to God. The Incarnation was a subject of eulogium to Mary because it was an indication of what she was in herself, not because of the physical relation with God which the Incarnation established. It was her inconceivable grace-fullness that captivated God. It is important to understand this. What was true of Mary up to the age of sixteen years, was true of her all her life long. Her gaze never rested on the human features of her Divine Child without her seeing through them the Divinity. Mary was always worshipping the Godhead in Her Son.

There is yet another corrective which is necessary to be applied. Office, as such, means nothing in God's sight. It is a great thing to be the Vicar of Christ on earth, yet if a simple, humble man has one degree of sanctity more than the Pope, he is far more preferable in God's eyes. Grace is the only thing worth while—the only thing of value in God's

[2] Luke i. 28.
[3] Luke xi. 28.
[4] Matt. xii. 48-50.

sight. Mothers often desire to have a son a priest; this desire
is laudable if they mean a holy priest, but a son not a priest,
who is one degree holier is much more preferable, Office
counts for nothing. This is true of Mary herself—the Mother
of God. We must think of the Incarnation only in terms of
Mary's interior life. It was at the time of the Annunciation
that Mary's true greatness was shown. We know how Mary
" was troubled "[5] at the Angel's message. We know, too, the
profound reason of her agitation. She was receiving an invitation to come closer to God, to enter into depths of mystical
life which are inconceivable to us, and Mary shrank back.
Try to realise that Mary's soul was one that had to progress
from day to day. It was this progress that *earned* for her in
Heaven a place above patriarchs and prophets, above angels
and saints, above even the burning cherubim and seraphim.
She earned this because of the divine life within her soul.
Mary was invited to occupy this lofty position and at the
same time she realised what the acceptance of this invitation
would cost nature. No wonder that mighty soul was troubled.
She saw the appalling depths of sacrifice that would be
wrought in her, not because of any sinfulness in herself, but
because of the mission she had to fulfil. She knew this sacrifice would be paid by the Flesh of her flesh, and Bone of her
bone. She knew the Scriptures and realised that from the
moment she uttered her " Fiat," that Child would be at once
her Joy and her Sorrow—both immeasurable. The Cross
was ever before her mind. Impending suffering is usually
harder than the actual suffering itself. Her Child was given
to her only to be torn from her later. Already she saw His
mangled Body, already she saw her Babe, laid on the Cross,
and at the sight, a chill like a dagger passed across her extremely sensitive soul. She was allowed to have no illusions.
When the Boy was but six weeks old, Simeon's prophecy
came to confirm what she already knew. " This Child is set
for the fall and for the resurrection of many in Israel .... and
thine own soul a sword shall pierce."[6] That is the price Mary
had to pay for her ascent to the Bosom of the Father—that
was the price of her title—" Mother of God." No wonder

[5] Luke i. 29.

[6] Luke ii. 34-35.

there was no room for an outburst of gladness at the declaration of her sinlessness. God was inviting her to come more close to Him, and acceptance of that invitation meant the Cross. It was a dreadful Cross to present to anyone so finely sensitive as Mary ; she was supersensitive and very young. No wonder Our Divine Lord corrected the woman who spoke up from the crowd. Mary's Motherhood of Jesus was a very small thing in comparison with becoming more divine at such a cost. Mary was free. She could have refused and still have remained a friend of God. True, she could not fall from grace but she could have failed to rise to the dizzy heights of sanctity now offered to her. In Mary, there is a complete absence of eagerness. The quietness of the scene cannot but impress us. When Mary has fully accepted, in an attitude of dignified calm she asks the angel, " How shall this be done, because I know not man?"[7] The angel then unfolds to her the mode—the power and operation of the Holy Ghost. Then Mary utters her " Behold the handmaid of the Lord."[8] Think of all that means in terms of reality. In the lives of all the saints there are moments parallel to this moment in Mary's life. The moments when the saints were faced with decisions fraught with momentous consequence for their whole spiritual life, are faint, though real images of Mary's position here. In other words, this is a scene in the mystical life of Mary. It is not merely a scene in the physical life of Our Divine Lord. Notice the courage, the fortitude of Mary when it is a question of God's good pleasure. Mary's reason told her that this act was pleasing to God and therefore because she loved God she consented. Her love of mankind also made her consent because her Child was to come as the Saviour of the human race. Mary is enthusiastic for God's glory and that enthusiasm nerved her to face the issue with fortitude. *Remember always* that Mary was a human being. She needed fortitude to face the cross. Again look at her Faith. The God she worshipped, the God Whom the Old Testament depicted for her as the Lord of Hosts and the God of Armies—this God of Might and Majesty become her Child! Tremendous thought, equalled only by the immen-

[7] Luke i. 34.
[8] Luke i. 38.

sity of her Faith. Her Faith stood the test. Oh! the wonderful simplicity of it all. Mary did not say "I am not worthy. Someone else would do better." She just abided by God's will. God Himself was, so to say, wrapped in admiration at her reaction and He gave expression to this admiration by the mouth of St. Elizabeth. Elizabeth in her enthusiasm cried aloud on meeting Mary: " Blessed art thou because thou has believed,"[9] and Mary calmly answered: " My soul doth magnify the Lord."[10] God recognised and appreciated at its true worth the great Faith of His handmaid.

We fail, however, both in Faith and Courage. Perhaps, today, God is asking us, as He asked Mary then, to come to a more intimate union with Him. We all have a number of such visitations in our life. God asks to be more perfectly born in us, in our souls. How do we comport ourselves on these occasions? Very poorly indeed! Our self-love stands in the way. God says to us: " You must give up this natural attachment. Give Me an undivided heart. Beware of antipathies. Give up breaking silence, it is mere self-indulgence. Bear bravely that difficulty in your work, and do not complain. Be more kind, more thoughtful, more courteous, more childlike, in a word, more Mary-like." We think that God is demanding far too much of us. It is too costly to nature. We persuade ourselves that He really does not mean it for us. Anyway, we say, being too holy makes things difficult for those with whom we live; it is not safe; better avoid extremes. The truth is that our Faith and Courage cannot stand these demands. We know what acceptance of God's invitation means, and we remain cowards and ungenerous. Mary accepted and she became the Mater Dolorosa. We persuade ourselves we are all right, and just remain where we are. We are satisfied to go on living a nice, comfortable and easy life, never rising above a state of mediocrity and continually wriggling out of every difficulty which demands self-sacrifice.

But let us take courage. Mary, with all her pain and suffering enjoyed happiness and joy unutterable. We feel unable to face the issue—let us ask Mary to help us. If our

9 Luke i. 45.

10 Luke i. 46.

desire is sincere, Mary *will* help us, and immense joy will be ours, even in the midst of suffering. And thus we shall share in Mary's real greatness, the greatness of all those who " hear the word of God and keep it."[11]

[11] Luke xi. 28.

CHAPTER XIII.

MARY MEDIATRIX OF ALL GRACES.

"He that shall find me, shall find life" (Prov. vii. 35).

There is yet a final mystery of our Faith, with which we are familiar already but which needs still further clarification if we are to make it a vitalising principle in our lives. Devotion to the Sacred Heart was known in the world all down the ages but it was only after the visions of St. Margaret Mary that it became widespread. I believe God will raise up another Saint who will teach us Mary's place in, and her influence on our supernatural life. This, it appears to me, will be the consummation of Christianity.

Mary is not an ornament—she is essential to our whole Christian life. No one, so far as I know, has yet fully elucidated her essential rôle—her true Motherhood in our spiritual life. There is an amount of literature on the subject. This I have studied, and have given the fruit of my thoughts in the last two chapters of " The True Vine and Its Branches." The result is far short of my desires and I know that much is yet to be said of the practical action of Mary on every human soul. She is Our Mother in the true and literal sense of the word and according to our realisation of her Motherhood is the degree of our Faith. If that filial attitude is strong our Faith is strong. Up to about sixty years ago this filial attitude was characteristic of the Irish people and since then it seems to be growing weak. " Mary—Mother " was everything to them. In her they confided for everything.

In the spiritual order we are infants in Mary's arms—*infants,* not even children. An infant must utterly depend on its mother for all things—nourishment, movement, clothing, washing. It is true that the father is the head of the family but the immediate care of the infant devolves on the mother. As the infant is in the natural order so are we in the supernatural order. Of course, the parallel has some limitations.

An infant can do nothing for himself. Does that mean that we are to sit back and do nothing? By no means! That would be to mistake the metaphor for the reality. To get at the exact position of Mary is difficult—the idea somehow evades us. We are unaware of this absolute dependence on her which really exists even though we do not realise it. As long as our spiritual life rests *exclusively* on Our Divine Lord we have not the right attitude and our growth in perfection will be retarded. This growth increases according as we realise Mary's place in the spiritual life of our souls. *Only* when Mary holds the *full field of consciousness* in our spiritual life will that life reach its full development. Although Christ is the Ultimate Source of the supply of our spiritual needs—Our Lady is in a very true sense the immediate source. If we put Our Lady on one side our spirituality is imperfect.

No one has yet elucidated fully Mary's rôle; so what are we to do? First of all, we should pray a great deal—pray to realise the essentiality of Mary's place in our lives. Note the word—*essentiality*. She is Our Mother in the full and literal meaning of the term. To her we owe everything in the supernatural order, as we do to our mother in the natural order. We know that since the sixteenth century Mary's rightful place has been denied her and that rejection of Mary was the beginning of all the evils in the world to-day. We have all met good Protestants but there is always a lack about their rectitude which jars on us. What makes their spirituality so harsh? It is the lack of Mary's Motherhood. A child, who loses its mother, before it has grown up, suffers an irreparable loss.

If Mary is to be Our Mother we must be her infant. It is a very difficult thing for us to become an infant. In an infant there is no self-will, no pride, no vanity. In many of their homilies the Fathers of the Church enumerate for us the qualities of a child. We remember the Gospel incident when Our Lord called a little child into the midst of the Apostles and taught them the lesson " Unless you be converted and become as little children you shall not enter into the Kingdom of Heaven."[1] The word used both in Greek and in Latin means

[1] Matt. xviii. 3.

a very young child, an infant, one who is still utterly dependent. The Apostles were very good men—even fit for canon-
isation according to our standards (which are never too high).
True they had some faults but these faults, though serious,
were not grave. They were holy men. Now Jesus tells them
they must become as little children. Severe discipline is necessary for conversion to the spiritual attitude symbolised by
that child placed in their midst. Such a conversion means
suppression of pride, vanity, self-will and self-consciousness.
St. Theresa of Lisieux was childlike and so were all the other
saints, in fact unless they were childlike they would not be
saints. This stage of spiritual childhood can only be reached
under Mary's influence. It means absolute self-denial— suppression of self. We always want to be " somebody "—
rather we want to be ourselves ; a child has none of these
desires. A child always wants to be " of somebody." Really
all our faults come from our self-centredness. This self-
centredness clearly manifests itself in our standards of evalua-
tion of persons and things. We say " so-and-so is a fine
character." Why? " Because he is good to me ; he does not
cross my path in any way ; he thinks as I do." It is always
" how the thing effects me " that weighs in our estimation of
character. " The impression made on me " is the source of
our motives for judging good or ill of a person's character.
Such a manner of estimating is far from being childlike. To
become childlike is a hard process ; it means wrestling with
every tendency in our being. We are all so well acquainted
with St. Paul's expression " the old man " that it no longer
seems strange to us. In the spiritual order we are born " old
men." At our birth we are aged, feeble and decrepit supernaturally. We are born old and to progress in holiness we
must come down—become young, childlike—and I say
"childlike " not " childish." Childishness consists in counting
of importance things which are not important. We are childish not childlike when we consider self as important ; when
we are hurt because we are wronged, treated unjustly, not
listened to or passed over. Every morning at Holy Mass we
pray to become as children, " ad Deum qui laetificat juventu-
tem meam." This process will only be completed when our
whole mentality is dominated by Our Mother Mary. When

her Motherhood occupies us completely then we become childlike. The mystery of Mary's Motherhood is profound, but it is very real, very true. Mary is indeed our Mother.

In this light we can see how unreal are our prayers for peace. They are unreal, because we cannot have peace without the cause of peace. Until the world assents to depend on its Mother Mary, whose Motherhood of Mankind was proclaimed on Calvary, there can be no peace. The Fall came through woman, and only through the Woman Mary, can we get back to God. Abandonment of Mary has left the world where it is. Mary is our only hope of peace. If we recognise her Motherhood, we shall have peace in our souls. If the world recognises her Motherhood there will be peace on earth. Women in the world to-day are unfaithful to this ideal. The loss of the ideal of womanhood, even in Catholic lands, has contributed notably to bring about the present grave disaster. How few girls have as their ideal of womanhood Our Blessed Lady? Strange as it may seem Mary makes more appeal in boys' schools than in girls'. Boys are more ready to listen when we speak of Our Lady. Talk to them about anything else and they will be restless, uneasy and cough at a great rate; but Mary always captivates their full attention. This is not the case with girls. Why? Well, the ideal of Mary is troublesome to girls. To uphold her would condemn their whole lives—their whole conduct and general outlook. If they adopted her as an Ideal they would have to change their lives and they do not want that. It would cost too much. That is the key to most of the unhappiness in the world. The world fell by Eve and only when Mary's rightful place, as Mother of men, is fully accepted will the world be able to rise. The recent apparitions of Our Lady at Fatima show us the truth of this wonderful doctrine. Mary is the Mediatrix of all Graces and it is through Mary alone, the grace of true peace among nations can come to the world. Justly then, in these days of turmoil and war does the Church salute Our Blessed Mother with the glorious title—" Mediatrix Potentissima."

" O Lord Jesus Christ, our Mediator with the Father, who hast been pleased to appoint the Most Blessed Virgin, Thy Mother, to be our Mother also and our Mediatrix with Thee, mercifully grant that whosoever comes to Thee seeking Thy favours, may rejoice to receive all of them through her. Amen."[2]

---

[2] Office of the Feast of Mary, Mediatrix of All Graces.

CHAPTER XIV.

MOTHER AND QUEEN.

*" And a great sign appeared in heaven, a woman clothed with
the sun, and the moon under her feet, and on her head a
crown of twelve stars "* (Apocalypse xii. 1).

Our Holy Mother the Church incessantly exhorts her
children to meditate with close attention on the great mystery
of our Redemption. It is a mystery that can never be fully
explored. It opens up boundless horizons before us as we
make it the object of our contemplation. Our mind, in its
actual condition, being obliged to see divine things in the
obscure light of faith, is not able to seize, in one comprehen-
sive glance, all the component parts of the divine plan for
the redemption of mankind. It is obliged to break up this
splendid unity, and to study in detail the several mysteries
which entered into the economy of redemption.

On the Cross, Christ accomplished the sacrifice of Himself.
By His sufferings and death on our behalf, He has made possible the redemption of all souls. On Calvary has been thrown
open once for all, these inexhaustible treasures of divine
grace, on which all men can draw, in order to work out their
salvation and to enter into their heavenly inheritance. Everything that, according to the mysterious designs of God, was
needed so that the grace of Christ should have its full
efficacy, was consummated on Calvary. But it is required, on
man's part, that he should have the dispositions needed to
profit by the grace thus won for him. Our salvation cannot
be worked out without our co-operation. Being endowed
with freedom we cannot be saved without our freely willing
our salvation. Christ opens the way to heaven for us ; we,
for our part, consent to walk in His footsteps. The graces
merited on Calvary must be applied to each individual soul.

The mode of application of these graces puts us in the presence of one of the most touching and most consoling mysteries of our Faith. Jesus, having associated His Mother with Him in carrying out the work of the Redemption, goes on to associate her with Him in carrying the Redemption into effect, in the sanctification of the individual soul. He has made her the mistress of the divine treasury and bestowed on her the office of distributing the divine gifts to all mankind. Mary is Mother of divine grace. She is our spiritual mother. She helps unceasingly the supernatural life to be conveyed to us. How touching is this truth of our faith, and how consoling for us who are so conscious of our spiritual helplessness. Who can describe the attractiveness, the charm, the power, the sweetness given to Christianity because of this all-prevailing atmosphere of Mary's supernatural Motherhood?

Mary is Mother of divine grace because it is she who has given us Him, in Whom grace dwells in its fulness, and Who is the Unique Source of all supernatural goods. But her rôle in the work of Redemption does not end there. By her " fiat " she became Mother of God, of a Divine Person Whose function it was to be a Saviour. By consenting to become Mother of the Word of God, Mary consented to become the Mother of Him, Who also, according to the divine plan, was preordained to be Head of the regenerated human race. The Personality of Jesus is indivisible. It is one and the same Person Who is the Word of God and the Head of regenerated mankind. Being Mother of the Head, she becomes the Mother of all the members united with the Head in the unity of a single Mystical Body. The " fiat " of the day of the Annunciation has effected in Mary a dual maternity. She became Mother of Jesus according to the flesh, and Mother of us according to the spirit. These two Motherhoods are intimately interwoven in the unity of the divine plan of the Redemption. They fundamentally constitute but a single Motherhood, that Motherhood from which springs the Complete Christ, the Head and Members of the Mystical Body.

The first function of a mother is to co-operate with God in giving life. Our life in the supernatural order has its source in and is the effect of sanctifying grace. Of course, the production of sanctifying grace cannot be attributed to the

Mother of God. This power of producing grace belongs to God alone. But surpassing all creatures as she does, in her sanctity and in the closeness of her union with Christ, and having been associated with her Son in the work of the Redemption of mankind, the Blessed Virgin has merited by divine favour or congruously, what her Son has merited in strict justice. As a consequence, she has been appointed by God, Dispensatrix of all graces. In the merciful designs of His Divine Providence, God has determined that Jesus and Mary should be associated together in all the phases of the Redemption. By her "fiat" our Blessed Lady accepted all that was implied in the divine plan. By this consent of hers, given with perfect freedom, she has become mediatrix between God and man, mediatrix at the throne of the Unique Mediator. In this way, as secondary and subordinate cause, she has merited for us the grace of Redemption which Jesus has merited as Principal Cause, for the mediation of Mary though subordinate to, and dependant on, that of Christ, enjoys the same universality as His. Mary's mediation extends to all men. Thus at the moment of the Annunciation Mary co-operated in acquiring for us the divine grace which is the life of our souls. In that supreme moment, we, being supernaturally conceived in her, became in very truth her children, and there commenced in our regard, Mary's rôle of spiritual Motherhood. It is often stated that Mary became our mother at the foot of the Cross. It is true that it was on Calvary the work of the Redemption was brought to a triumphant issue, but the mission of Jesus and Mary, which was consummated on Calvary, began at Nazareth. With her "fiat" of Nazareth, Mary became our Mother, but it was at the foot of the Cross that her spiritual Maternity received its full perfection. There, we, her children, were brought forth in pain. By the sacrifice of the Cross Jesus finally effected our deliverance and won for us salvation. By that sacrifice mankind recovered the supernatural life it had lost. On Calvary, the price of our regeneration was paid in all its fullness, and it was on Calvary that Mary took her definite place in the scheme of the Redemption. There the Mystical Body took form; there the life of the Head was made available to the members. There Mary became, in fullest sense, Mother of the Complete Christ.

Mary has given us the Author and Source of all grace. She has brought us forth to supernatural life. But this does not exhaust all the meaning in her title of Mother of Divine Grace. A mother not only begets children, she nourishes them as well. She guides their first steps. She rears them and presides at their formation until they attain to manhood. When the child is hurt it runs to its mother. It is she who applies healing remedies. So too is it in the spiritual life. Mary not only brings us to birth supernaturally, she gives as well all that is required to nourish, develop and perfect this supernatural life in us. So true is this that, according to the ordinary teaching of the Church, all graces come to us through the intercession and mediation of Mary. Through her reach us all the treasures acquired by Jesus for the salvation of men. St. Bernard says it is God's will that all good from heaven should come to us at Mary's hands. In the course of ages this doctrine has been consistently confirmed by the Doctors, Saints and Theologians who have preached it and committed it to writing. "Thanks to the mutual interchange of love and pain between Jesus and Mary," says the holy Pope Pius X, "Mary rightly deserves to be the Restorer of the fallen human race, the great Mediatrix of the whole world and, as a consequence, the Distributor of all the supernatural riches Jesus has acquired for us by the shedding of His Precious Blood." (Encyc. Diem Illum, Pius X).

These words of Pope Pius X, placing Mary before us as Universal Distributor of the gifts of God and Mother of Divine Grace, should inspire our devotion to our Blessed Lady. Devotion to Mary is not a devotion which we are completely free to practice or to leave aside at will. Every Christian who wishes to fall in with the divine plan is bound to practise it. Mary is in practice an essential factor in the spiritual life. Without Jesus no salvation, without Mary no Jesus. And as without Mary it is impossible to have Jesus, so too without a knowledge of Mary it is impossible to have a knowledge of Jesus. This is the reason why, wherever the Mother of God is kept out of view, wherever she is unknown and neglected, enlightened and right knowledge of the nature and mission of the Man-God tends to diminish and disappear. The cause of all the heresies that have ravaged the Church, the explanation of all failures in the spiritual life, can be traced to, and discovered in a lack of recognition of the spiritual Maternity of Mary.

Mary is our Mother: she is Mother of God. In this Maternity of Mary lies the greatest manifestation of the divine goodness. In the natural order there is nothing greater, deeper, or stronger than the mutual love of mother and child. God, in His divine wisdom, has implanted the same mutual love in the supernatural order. " In every manner," says St. Bernard, " God wishes to calm our fears, to excite our confidence, to strengthen our hopes, banish our distrust and encourage our timidity. If you are afraid to approach the Father you have Jesus for Mediator. If you shrink before the divine Majesty in Jesus, Who though man, remains God, there is provided for you an advocate with the Saviour Himself. For it is open to you to have recourse to Mary. Of a certainty, the Son will hear the prayer of the Mother. There is the unshakeable ground for your hope."

Mary has given to the Redemption a " cachet " of graciousness and tenderness, of adaptation to and correspondence with the instincts and needs of our nature. Jesus has created in her heart a mother's love for us, which is surpassed only by that which she bears for her divine Son. Nay rather, her love for us is identified with her love for Jesus. She is our Mother, we can have recourse to her in all confidence. As Mother of Jesus her intercession with Him is all-powerful. He can refuse nothing to her whom He loves with the boundless love of His Sacred Heart. If we draw near to her trustfully, we are sure of being heard. She will not always take the cross from our shoulders, but she will show us how to carry it. She will not always wipe away our tears, but she will show us how to unite them with her own and those of Jesus. She will obtain for us a share in the joy and peace which were hers in the midst of her grief and anguish.

When Almighty God predestined Jesus for the work of our Redemption, He also predestined to be associated with Jesus in the world's salvation, the privileged creature by whom the Saviour was to make His entry into the world. In the divine

plan, Mary is indissolubly associated with her Son, the Word
Incarnate, in accomplishing the salvation of mankind. It is
because of this, that Mary makes her appearance at the very
beginning of the Old Testament. She is found too at the
inauguration of the New Alliance. When the fullness of time
had come for the accomplishment of the great mystery, the
Eternal Splendour of the Father, begotten before the dawn
of time, appeared on the earth. The first worshippers set out
to seek and to adore Him, Whose star had appeared in the
East. What did they find? "Entering into the house they
found the Child with Mary His Mother."[1]

These simple words do not merely relate a historical fact;
they express a principle and ennunciate a law. This principle,
this law of things in the economy of salvation, is recalled by
the Sacred Writer, at the supreme moment, when the redeem-
ing sacrifice was about to be consummated. "There stood
by the Cross of Jesus, His Mother."[2] On the hill of Calvary
the Mediatrix took her stand by the side of the Unique
Mediator.

Indissolubly united in the mystery of the Incarnation,
mysteriously identified in the mystery of the Redemption, is
it surprising to find Jesus and Mary everlastingly associated
in the mystery of glorification? At Bethlehem, Jesus was
found with Mary, His Mother ; on Golgotha, Mary as "Co-
redemptress" stood at the foot of the Cross of Jesus, the
Redeemer ; in the state of triumphant glory, Jesus as King,
places at his side, Mary, Queen of Heaven.

This glorification of Mary is a truth held throughout all
Christendom. The Church unhesitatingly places the Queen
by the side of the King of glory, since it knows that Mary, in
virtue of her Assumption, is in the same place and in the
same state that Jesus enjoys in virtue of His Ascension. When
the term of her exile in the valley of tears had come, the
Immaculate Virgin, peacefully breathed forth her most holy
soul in one great sigh of divine love. "Just as the slightest
breath detaches the fully ripe fruit from a tree ; just as a
flame, of its own accord, mounts upwards and seeks its proper

[1] Matt. ii. 11.

[2] John xix. 25.

altitude, so this stainless soul was taken from earth to be borne straight to Heaven."[3] Instructed by an unquestioned and unbroken tradition, we can, with the Apostles gathered at Ephesus, contemplate with eyes of faith, the Blessed Virgin mounting heavenwards. Our faith allows us to follow her in spirit and to catch some gleams of the light which transpierces the veil surrounding the Heavenly Jerusalem. The whole of heaven moves joyously forward to the threshold of the Heavenly Court to receive their Queen. The Eternal Father welcomes with great love, the fairest flower of all His creations. The Holy Spirit murmurs in tender accents: "Arise, make haste, my love, my dove, my beautiful one, and come, for winter is now past, the rain is over and gone."[4]

And St. John, the holy seer of Patmos, reveals to us Jesus, her Divine Son as He advances to meet His Mother. Jesus then seats Himself on His throne and causes a throne to be set for His Mother, who takes her place at His right hand. Henceforth she shares all His distinction, all His power, all His majesty. The piercing vision of the great contemplative of Patmos, reveals her as Queen of Heaven, in all the glory of her state. "And a great sign appeared in heaven; a woman clothed with the sun, and the moon under her feet, and on her head a crown of twelve stars."[5] The Queen Mother is seated by the side of the King, her Son.

Mary, Our Queen and our Mother, pray for us, intercede for us with thy Divine Son, Our Lord, Jesus Christ.

---

[3] Bossuet.
[4] Canticle of Canticles ii. 10, 11.
[5] Apoc. xii. 1.

PART II.

THE IMMACULATE HEART OF MARY.

By Rev. John Kearney, C.S.Sp.

" In me is all hope of Life."
(Eccles. xxiv).

CHAPTER I.

NATURE OF DEVOTION TO THE IMMACULATE HEART OF MARY.

" All the glory of the King's Daughter is within."

(Ps. xliv. 14.)

INTRODUCTION.

He who would write of the Mother of God must make his own these beautiful words of St. Basil of Seleucia:

" Can there be any subject more sublime than this? He who thinks so has not understood the difference between things human and things divine. For as it is not easy to know God and to speak of Him, yea, rather it is among the things that can least be done ; so the great mystery of the Mother of God transcends both speech and reason. When then I speak of the Mother of God incarnate, I will ascend to God by the help of prayer, and will seek Him for the guide of my speech, and will say to Him: ' O Lord Omnipotent, King of all creation, who in an incomprehensible manner dost infuse Thy spiritual light into incorporeal minds, illuminate my mind, that the subject set before me may be understood without error ; may, when understood, be spoken with piety, and when spoken, may be received without hesitation.'

" O God, Who hath given us to venerate the Most Blessed Virgin Mary, Queen of all Saints, and Mother of Fair Love: grant in Thy kindness that with her protection, we may love thee in all and above all while on earth, and enjoy the blissful companionship of Thy Saints in heaven. Through Christ Our Lord," Amen.

§ I.

THE MEANING OF THE WORD "HEART"

Our human life depends, in a special way, on the perfect functioning of our heart. On account of the work done by this organ, if its movement is stopped, circulation of the blood ceases and death follows. Although the heart, in accordance with God's design, drives the blood, by its pulsation, to every minute part of our body, it does so without our being aware of this fact. Unadverted to by us, day and night, incessant in its beat, it sends the life-giving blood to our brain, to the delicate mysterious structure of our eyes and ears, and to the muscles by which we can move ourselves.

But the heart, which, by its natural movement, controls the flow of our blood, is itself influenced by the thoughts of our mind, by the acts of our will, and by the movements of our emotional nature. Its beat, although never ceasing, is slower or faster, stronger or weaker, according as our senses are impressed, and according as our mind, our will and our feelings react to these impressions.

From the fact of this reaction between soul and body has come the usage of speaking of the human heart in a moral sense. The heart is considered as being most intimately related to all the dispositions and movements both good and bad of our soul. Thus the word "heart" is used not merely in reference to the various acts but also in reference to the various states of the human spirit. Finally, in ordinary language the word "heart" has come to be used as if it were the very seat of the movements, acts and dispositions of our soul.

Hence it is that when we wish to speak of any or of all the internal activities or dispositions of a soul, of the complex of qualities that go to make up a character, we naturally use the word "heart."

Thus we speak of a hard heart, a cold heart, a selfish heart, a cruel heart. We also speak of a kind heart, a good heart, a generous heart, a loving heart, a tender heart, a contrite heart, a broken heart, a sorrowful heart.

These examples show us that the word "heart" in ordinary usage means the soul with its dispositions, good and bad, its virtues and its vices.

But we should keep in mind that the heart is not a mere symbol of these interior dispositions and acts of the soul: it responds to them, it beats in sympathy with them, it is so affected by them that we can say it participates in them.

The word " heart ", then, stands for the interior life of the soul ; it also stands for the person with all the characteristics, the virtues or vices that that person has.

§ II.

THE WORD " HEART " IN THE HOLY SCRIPTURE.

The Holy Scripture, both in the Old Testament and in the New uses the word " heart " in the sense we have explained above, i.e., as meaning the dispositions and acts of the soul.

It is so used a great many times in the Psalms: here are some examples:—

" To-day if you shall hear His voice, harden not your *hearts*." (Ps. 94.)

" My *heart* is become like wax melting." (Ps. 21.)

" My *heart* shall not fear." (Ps. 26).

" The thoughts of his *heart* stand to all generations." (Ps. 32.)

" He knoweth the secrets of the *heart*." (Ps. xliii. 22.)

Examples of this usage are also very numerous in the other books of the Old Testament:—

" The *heart* of Pharao was hardened." (Exod. vii. 13.)

" At this my *heart* trembleth." (Job xxxvii.)

In the New Testament *Our Lord Himself* uses the word " heart " in the same sense:

" Learn of Me for I am meek and humble of *heart*." (Matt xi. 29.)

The word "heart" as here used clearly means the dispositions of the beautiful soul of Jesus in which were the virtues of humility and meekness.

There are many examples of the same usage:—

"Let not your *heart* be troubled." (John xiv l).

"Where your treasure is, there is your *heart* also." (Matt. vi 21.)

"This people honoureth Me with their lips; but their *heart* is far from Me." (Matt. xv 8.)

"Was not our *heart* burning within us whilst He spoke to us in the way?" (Luke xxiv. 32.)

"From the abundance of the *heart* the mouth speaketh." (Matt. xii. 34.)

"He grieved over the blindness of their *heart.*" (Mark iii. 5.)

"Because I have spoken these things to you sorrow hath filled your *heart.*" (John xvi. 6.)

"Blessed are the clean of *heart.*" (Matt v.)

"You shall love the Lord Thy God with all your *heart.*" (St. Luke x. 27.)

"O foolish and slow of *heart* to believe," (Luke xxiv. 25.)

"It has not entered into the *heart* of man to conceive what God has prepared for those that love Him." (1 Cor. ii. 9.)

In the above quotations the word "heart" is obviously synonymous with soul or disposition of soul.

The Church has adopted the same use of the word "heart."

The introduction to the Preface at Holy Mass includes these words:—"Lift up your *hearts*"—"Sursum corda."

In the Gradual of the Mass of Pentecost Sunday we have this appeal:—"Come, O Holy Ghost, fill the *hearts* of Thy faithful, and enkindle in them the fire of Thy love."

In the Mass to implore the grace of the Holy Ghost the Church prays:—" O God, to Whom all *hearts* are open and every will doth speak, and from Whom no secret lies concealed, purify, by the infusion of the Holy Spirit the thoughts of our *hearts,* that we may merit perfectly to love and worthily to praise Thee, through Christ Our Lord."

And again:—

" May the grace of the Holy Spirit, we beseech Thee, Lord, illuminate our *hearts,* and with delight of perfect charity abundantly refresh them. Through Christ Our Lord. Amen."

And in another Collect:—" Direct to Thyself, we beseech Thee, O God, the *hearts* of Thy servants that, being inflamed with the fire of Thy Holy Spirit, they may be found both firm in faith and zealous in good deeds. Through Christ Our Lord. Amen."

Thus the Church, in her Liturgy uses the word " heart "— as Our Lord did—to mean the soul with its acts and dispositions. Falling from the lips of Christ and expressed in the Church's liturgy the word is used to mean the soul with its acts and dispositions.

§ III.

THE HOLY HEART OF MARY.

The truths we have considered enable us to have a fuller knowledge of the Holy Heart of Mary, the Mother of Jesus.

She had a perfect human nature, the most perfect ever created, excepting the human nature of her Divine Son. There was a perfect balance and delicacy in all her physical powers.

Her body was perfect in every way—from it the Holy Ghost formed the Sacred Body of Jesus. That body was, in consequence, perfectly fitted to be moved and influenced by the movements of her most beautiful soul, and hence was exquisitely sensitive.

The heart of Mary drove the streams of her blood to every part of her immaculate body and reacted with unimaginable delicacy to every movement of her most holy soul—a soul whose sanctity not even the angelic minds can perfectly grasp. This physical perfection was the result of a particular providence. God Himself, in a most special way, watched over all the series of Mary's ancestry: He guided all the physical laws that are related to the mysterious question of heredity, so that while the good was preserved defects of character were not transmitted. Thus the body of Mary, by these very laws which God directed, was possessed of a perfection of temperament and character that made it fit to receive the most beautiful soul that God had yet created. We all know from experience that the heart of an ordinary human being does not respond perfectly to the movements of the soul. Thus we may be real lovers of God and yet our physical heart may not respond; we feel nothing, as we say; we are not directly conscious of our love.

In the case of Our Lady it was not so. Her organism was so perfect that her Holy Heart responded perfectly to every act and disposition of her soul. She felt her love for her Son, and She felt her love for men.

These fundamental truths give us a fuller understanding of the Heart of Mary, which was so perfectly prepared to respond in sympathy with the least movement of her soul. The soul of Mary was of unimaginable natural beauty, of indescribably perfect dispositions, and was lifted by her grace above the natural plane to a perfection that God alone can comprehend. All this leads us to wish to know more of this admirable soul.

§ IV.

HOW WE CAN KNOW THE HOLY HEART OF MARY.

But perhaps we may question, we may even have doubts about the possibility of knowing the Heart of Mary, that is, about the possibility of knowing her interior life, her hidden dispositions, the intimate secrets of her beautiful soul. The Scripture seems to say so little about the *exterior* life of Our Lady, how then can we know her *interior* life? how can we penetrate into the secrets of her holy heart?

The answer is that, without drawing on our imagination,

we *can reach* a true knowledge of this admirable Heart. If we bring together what the infallible Church has said of the soul of Mary, and what the Holy Scripture has said about her, the various items in both these series of statements throw light one on another. And the patient investigating and contrasting of them in the light of the principles of theology, will result in a knowledge of such accuracy as may well surprise those who have not made such a study.

But to penetrate into the secrets contained in the Holy Scripture and in the official words of the Church, we need abundant grace, we need the illumination that grace alone gives. We should ask this grace from Our Lady herself. She will surely grant our prayers, because she wishes her children to know her holy heart that they may have more confidence in her motherly care of them. From this knowledge there flows the true devotion to the Holy Ghost.

§ V.

DEVOTION TO THE HEART OF MARY.

When we speak of being devoted to another person, we mean being ready to do all we can to please the person, whose interests have become ours.

In like manner, when we are devoted to the Holy Mother of Jesus, it means that we have given our affections to her, and that we are desirous to please her, to promote her interests, to lead others to venerate her and love her.

Devotion means the promptitude of the will in the service of another—in promoting the interests of another.

Now when we are devoted to the Holy Heart of Mary, we are devoted to Mary herself.

Devotion to the admirable soul of Mary means devotion to *Mary Herself,* but to Mary regarded as possessing, and being, all that is beautiful, all that is perfect, as having all the qualities that go to make a human being absolutely lovable. In a most particular way then, the ultimate object of devotion to the Holy Heart of Mary is Mary herself the Holy Mother of Jesus, considered as characterized especially by her love for Jesus, her divine Son, and for us her spiritual children.

We shall now consider, and, with all reverence, explore and search into the secrets of the most beautiful soul of the Mother of God. This research, with God's grace, will make us more devoted to her.

The knowledge we shall reach of this admirable Heart means the knowledge of the most sweet character of Our Lady, it means the knowledge of her motherly tenderness, it means the knowledge of herself as all-beautiful, all-glorious all-kind, all-merciful and all-powerful to help, and hence as most inspiring, most comforting and most lovable.

Those who study and consider and contemplate the Holy Heart cannot but be devout children of Mary, and fair copies, as far as weakness allows, of their heavenly Mother. They have seen and known what Mary is like, and they will always strive to be like Mary.

But before we begin the study of the Holy Heart of Mary we shall give an account of the history of the devotion. When did it spring up in the Church? Who were the chosen souls that promoted it? And what were the signs that showed Our Lady's approval of their efforts?

"THE HOLY HEART OF MARY"

THE DEVOTION TO THE HOLY HEART OF MARY.

POINTS FOR PRAYER.

I.   The Meaning of the Word "HEART."

II.   The Word "HEART" in the Holy Scripture.

III.   The Holy Heart of Mary.

IV.   How we can know the Holy Heart of Mary.

V.   Devotion to the Heart of Mary.

CHAPTER II.

HISTORY OF THE DEVOTION TO THE IMMACULATE HEART OF MARY.

" All generations shall call me blessed."
(Luke i. 48.)

INTRODUCTION.

In the history of the Church we find that, as the years passed, God, in His goodness, has directed the thoughts of her rulers and her subjects to different points in the treasures of the revelation given to her. According as the Catholic mind in its development and in its needs was ready to profit by the more complete understanding of Catholic doctrine, God inspired His saints to consider more profoundly some point in the tradition of the Faith. The work begun by one saint on this particular point was perfected by another, and so on until these explanations and deductions were submitted to the infallible judgment of the Church. And thus under the guidance of the Holy Spirit, the Church has considered and explored one after another many of the secrets of God hidden in the depths of the fundamental truths of Christianity.

It is in this way that some of the hidden riches—the inexhaustible riches—of Catholic dogma became better known to the faithful. Thus souls are drawn to God, the Source of every good, and thus they are led to love more fervently Him Whose perfections are revealed more clearly every time a soul penetrates deeper into the Catholic Revelation.

A striking example of this opening-up of spiritual secrets is the development of devotion to the Sacred Heart of Jesus and to the Holy Heart of Mary. Considering especially the growth of the devotion to the Heart of the Mother of Jesus we find that the outstanding personality in the history of this devotion is St. John Eudes.

116

§ I.

ST. JOHN EUDES.

St. John Eudes was one of the great saints of the seventeenth century. He was born in Normandy, and lived his life almost exclusively in the North-West of France. He founded the Congregation of Jesus and Mary for priests—they are called the Eudists—and from him we have also the Sisters of Charity of Refuge, and the Sisters of the Good Shepherd. Holy Church gives us a short account of St. John Eudes both in the office of the Saint and in the Office of the Sacred Heart of Jesus. She tells us that he was the Father, the Doctor and the Apostle of the Liturgical devotion to the hearts of Jesus and Mary.

He was the Father of the Liturgical devotion because he took care that, in the Congregations he founded, these Feasts should be celebrated with great splendour. He was the Doctor because he composed the special Masses and the special offices of the Sacred Heart of Jesus and of the Holy Heart of Mary. He was the Apostle because he did all in his power to spread devotion to these Sacred Hearts.

Born in 1600, and dying in 1680, he accomplished this great work about the middle of the seventeenth century—in the year 1650. Although St. John Eudes was the first to organise and to spread the liturgical devotion to the Sacred Heart of Jesus, his labours were confined to a small part of the Catholic world. He was chosen to begin the devotion, but he was not chosen to spread the devotion over the whole world. For this Our Lord selected, some years later, in 1675, St. Margaret Mary to whom He appeared and to whom He explained the characteristics of the devotion, and whom He commanded to spread it. We know with what magnificent results she obeyed that command.

But to St. John Eudes and to the Congregation he founded was reserved the privilege of explaining the character of and of preserving and spreading the devotion to the Holy Heart of Mary. If we confidently ask the intercession of St. John Eudes, he will surely obtain for us special grace to understand the true nature of devotion to the Holy Heart of Mary.

§ II.

THE DEVOTION TO THE HOLY HEART OF MARY IN THE DISTANT PAST.

For long centuries before St. John Eudes, many saintly persons had venerated, spoken of, and written about the interior life of Mary, the life of her holy soul. Some few had spoken of the Heart of Mary as related in a special way to that holy soul with all the virtue it possessed. In writing thus, they were inspired no doubt by the usage of Holy Scripture.

But this devotion to the Holy Heart of Mary was found only among certain privileged souls who had the grace to penetrate deeply into the secrets of the life of Our Lady. The devotion was not public, it had no special approbation, it had no place in the Liturgy. An instance of this private devotion to the Holy Heart is found in the Revelations of St. Mechtilde who lived in the thirteenth century. We read (lib. i. cap. lxv) that it was granted to that Saint to honour and salute the Heart of the Blessed Virgin for seven special reasons:—

  I. On account of the ardent desires it conceived for the coming of Jesus Christ.

  II. On account of the love with which it burns, and because of its deep humility.

  III. On account of its tender love for the Infant Jesus.

  IV. For the care with which it treasured up the words of Jesus Christ.

  V. For its sufferings in the Passion of Jesus Christ.

  VI. On account of the prayers it offered up and the desires it formed for the Church.

  VII. On account of the care it takes in Heaven to make the Holy Trinity propitious to us.

(Fr. Gallifet, p. 255).

(i)

St Bernardine of Sienna, in the early years of the fifteenth century, preached and wrote about the Heart of Mary. St. John Eudes, in his office of the Holy Heart, took the lessons of the Second Nocturn from one of St. Bernardine's sermons.

St. Francis de Sales, in the beginning of the seventeenth century, spoke about the Heart of Mary, and in the crest of the Visitation Order which he founded, he placed the Hearts of Jesus and Mary united together. He also gives us a beautiful study of the holy soul of Our Lady in his treatise on the Love of God.

All the above instances of devotion to Our Lady's Heart were but the beginning, among the Saints, of the knowledge of the treasures hidden in that Holy Heart.

§ III.

THE EARLY YEARS OF THE LITURGICAL DEVOTIONS.

It was reserved to St. John Eudes to explain, as a theologian, the reason of the devotion, to establish the Feast, both in his own Congregations and in certain dioceses of France, with the approval of their Bishops, and to compose the special Mass and the special Office which are still used in his Congregations.

It is his great glory to have grasped before anyone else the full meaning and the theological basis of the devotion, and to have devoted himself to its establishment and to its spread. Here are some facts regarding the spread of the twofold devotion[1] : —

" The first Church dedicated to the Heart of Jesus (that of the Seminary of Coutances in Normandy) was at the same time jointly dedicated to the Heart of Mary. In 1688 a solemn feast with an octave was celebrated in that Seminary in honour of the Sacred Hearts, and even before that time a confraternity was established there under the title of the Confraternity of the Hearts of Jesus and Mary. On October 4th, 1674, in the fifth year of his Pontificate, Pope Clement X. honoured it with a Brief of Indulgences."

" Clement IX had already granted, on April 8th, 1668, a similar favour in honour of the Heart of Mary to the royal

[1] The extracts that follow are taken from the well-known book: " The Adorable Heart of Jesus," by Fr. Galliffet, S.J. This book published in 1726 brings us back to within a few years of the beginning of the liturgical devotions to the Sacred Heart of Jesus and the Holy Heart of Mary.

Abbey of Saint-Cesaire at Arles, where the feast is celebrated each year on the third Sunday after Pentecost.

" In 1654 the House of Refuge at Dijon was dedicated to the Sacred Heart of Mary.

" At Paris the Abbey of Montmartre and the Convent of the Nuns of the Blessed Sacrament have the right of celebrating the feast of the Heart of Mary with its Office, and all the solemnities of the greatest feasts, by authority of their Lordships, the Archbishops, and of a Legate *a Latere* of the Holy See.

" In 1668 the Friars Minor of the great province of France obtained permission from the Papal Legate to celebrate the Office of the Heart of Mary, as may be seen in their proper Offices."

In the life[1] of St. John Eudes, we find further details of his work in spreading the devotion to the Holy Heart of Mary. As early as 1648, with the approval of the Bishop, he had a public feast of the Holy Heart of Mary celebrated in Autun.

The approval was followed by that of many other Bishops. For St. John Eudes, the Holy Heart of Mary was the pivot of his spiritual life. Those who study his life can see how Our Lady led him to the highest holiness. She has done the same for many others, and will continue to lead the clients of her Holy Heart to the Heart of her Son.

§ IV.

THE WRITINGS OF ST. JOHN EUDES.

To spread the devotion to the Holy Heart of Mary, St. John Eudes preached and established feasts with episcopal approbation, but he also wrote many works great and small, all of which breathe his theological precision and his tender piety.

Because the devotion to the Sacred Heart of Jesus and the Holy Heart of Mary was drawing souls to a childlike love of God, and a tender confidence in His goodness, our Saint was bitterly and persistently attacked by the Jansenists.

We shall call to notice only two of the saint's works. The first great work, written specially in honour of the Holy Heart,

---

[1] By Henry Joly, p. 178.

was the Breviary Office and the Mass for the Feast of the Holy Heart of Mary. These were composed about 1641, and they are still used by the religious Societies that look to the saint as their founder—the priests of the Congregation of Jesus and Mary, the Sisters of Charity of Refuge and the Sisters of the Good Shepherd.

To spread the devotion to the Holy Heart of Mary our Saint, in addition, composed his great work entitled " The Admirable Heart of the Most Sacred Mother of God." This monument of his knowledge and devotion consists of twelve books; it runs to some 800 pages, and is characterised, like his other works, by its theological accuracy and its sincere and enthusiastic piety.

We give one passage:—

" When, therefore, we honour the Sacred Heart of the Mother of God we honour the Heart that, of all hearts, after the Heart of her Son, is the most worthy of our admiration, the most perfect, the most beloved by God, the most adorned with every kind of virtue, the most full of grace and love; the Heart that has most tenderness for poor sinners, that is the meekest, the most compassionate, the most merciful, the most charitable, the most beneficient, the most amiable; in a word, the object that, after Jesus, has the greatest charms for heaven and earth. It is, therefore, for the best of reasons that we should make this Sacred Heart of Mary the object of our tenderest devotion, and pay it all the honour and respect that its own excellence, and the favours we have received from it, demand of our gratitude and love."

A remarkable characteristic of the devotion of St. John Eudes is that he associated the Holy Heart of Mary so intimately with the Sacred Heart of Jesus—knowing how grace had made her Heart so like His.

Our Lady herself has shown her approval of this idea in the revelation of the Miraculous Medal of which we shall speak later. Let us ask Our Lady to lead us so to know her Holy Heart that we may know it as one with the Sacred Heart of Jesus.

§ V.

DIFFICULTIES IN THE XVIII CENTURY.

From the death of St. John Eudes (1680) until the French Revolution (1789), the devotion to the Holy Heart of Mary was preserved by the Eudists in the North West of France. But owing to the difficulties of the time and to the anti-Catholic forces at work in France, and especially to the enmity of the Jansenists, the sons of St. John could not develop the devotion outside the country of its origin.

The devotion to the Holy Heart was also preserved and developed by the writings of St. John and by many holy souls for whom it had a special appeal.

The persecutions of the French Revolution were so severe that they practically ruined the organisation of the Congregation of Jesus and Mary and scattered its members.

Among the victims of the Revolution, the Eudists count three martyred priests.

In the early years of the nineteenth century the surviving Eudist Fathers got together to begin the revival and reorganisation of the Congregation of Jesus and Mary.

It was a time of great trial. The French Revolution was followed by the wars of Napoleon which drew away the young manhood of France. These wars were followed by repeated revolutions. Everything was upset. Vocations were very few. But Our Lady blessed the work of the Eudist Fathers which was to spread devotion to her Holy Heart. She blessed their efforts at reorganisation, and their Congregation, now perfectly restored, is doing great work for the Church, the Mystic Body of the Son of Mary.

Gratitude for the preservation of this devotion is awakened when we consider the vicissitudes of the eighteenth century. We should ask Our Lady to save her children today from the dangers of a godless, materialistic world. In devotion to her Holy Heart will they find refuge, guidance and strength.

§ VI.

BLESSED CATHERINE LABOURÉ.

In the early nineteenth century Our Lady gave several very striking proofs of her desire that the veneration of her Holy Heart should be spread among the faithful, knowing as she did, the precious graces that would come to those of her children who cultivated the devotion. These proofs we shall now consider.

In the year 1830 the Holy Mother of Jesus gave a great impulse to the spread of the devotion to her Holy Heart by appearing to Blessed Catherine Labouré, a member of the Sisters of Charity, founded by St. Vincent de Paul. To this privileged soul Our Lady gave a vision of the Miraculous Medal and told her that she would give great graces to all who wore this medal. As we all know, one face of the medal represents the Heart of Jesus and Mary, side by side, thus symbolising their intimate union.

Blessed Catherine told her director of the vision, and he, after some prudent delay, got the medal approved. The Devotion spread widely, and marvellous were the graces brought by the medal—hence its name, The Miraculous Medal.

But Blessed Catherine kept until her death the secret of her vision and of her conversations with the Mother of God —a marvellous manifestation of humility and prudence. Of Our Lady it is written in reference to the hidden life of Jesus that " Mary kept all these words, pondering them in her heart " (Luke ii. 19). She did not speak of the mysteries or of her own privilege. Blessed Catherine imitates Our Lady. This humble soul will help those who find it hard to keep silence.

Blessed Catherine was ordered by her director to ask Our Blessed Lady what words should be inscribed on the face of the medal on which the images of the Hearts of Jesus and Mary were stamped. She was answered that no words were needed. The union of the two Hearts told all that was to be learned.

The union of the Sacred Heart of Jesus and the Holy Heart of Mary fills the mind with thoughts that are too deep for words.

§ VII.

THE IMMACULATE HEART OF MARY: REFUGE OF SINNERS: OUR LADY OF VICTORIES.

A few years after the revelation of the Miraculous Medal Our Lady gave further evidence that the devotion to her Holy Heart is most pleasing to her. In a large and very irreligious parish in Paris, the Parish Priest, Fr. Desgenettes, was continually praying that God would bless his efforts for his poor misgu:ded people. His church bore already the name of Our Lady of Victories. He looked to her, the Mother of Jesus, for help.

In December 1836, as he was making his thanksgiving after Mass, he heard a voice saying: " Consecrate your parish to the Holy Heart of Mary." He did so, and organised a Sodality under the title of " The Immaculate Heart of Mary, Refuge of Sinners," whose special object was prayers for the conversion of souls lost in the ways of sin.

The graces that followed were marvellous. The Parish was reformed. The Sodality spread over the whole Christian world. Everyone who visits the centre of the Arch-confraternity in the Church of Our Lady of Victories, Paris, will see the walls of the spacious Church covered with small marble slabs, each bearing the account of some miracle testifying to the motherly kindness of the Holy Heart of Mary.

The stream of favours flows increasingly from the Immaculate Heart of Mary, Refuge of Sinners. In that stream, we and all sinners may confidently seek the graces we need. Among those who frequented the Church of Our Lady of Victories about this time was an humble seminarist, a devout client of the Holy Heart, who was later to found a religious Missionary Congregation dedicated to the same Holy Heart.

§ VIII.

THE MISSIONERS OF THE HOLY HEART OF MARY: VEN. FR. LIBERMANN.

In 1841, five years after the founding of the Sodality of the Immaculate Heart of Mary, Refuge of Sinners, the Venerable Francis Libermann founded the *Missioners of the Holy*

Heart of Mary, which was, some years later, united to the Society of the Holy Ghost. The united Societies were called the Congregation of the Holy Ghost and of the Immaculate Heart of Mary.

How the Ven. Libermann was led to consecrate his young missioners to the Holy Heart of Mary we shall now briefly relate.

In the thirties of the 19th Century we find Venerable Francis Libermann, while yet but a student in Theology, placed in charge of the Novitiate of the Eudist Fathers. He was debarred from the priesthood by epilepsy, but his spiritual prudence and knowledge of the ways of holiness had led to his being placed in charge of the novices.

In this position he steeped his soul in the writings of St. John Eudes, and learned there the secrets of the Holy Heart of Mary.

Our Lady guided him thus to learn these secrets at the very fountain head, because he was destined to found a Society of Missionaries dedicated to her Holy Heart. Although he did much good and was greatly venerated as Master of Novices, yet guided by the hand of God, he decided to surrender his position of authority. This he did in order that he might be able to give his help to two clerical students from the French colonies who, knowing the absolute spiritual abandonment of the black workers in those colonies, were striving to found a Society of Priests to bring them the blessing of the Faith.

We next find Francis Libermann at Rome where he had gone to submit to the Propaganda the project of founding such a Society. While there, he had to draw up a rule for the future Congregation. He himself tells us that he could make no progress with the rule until the inspiration came to him to consecrate the future Congregation to the Holy Heart of Mary. Once he had done this he drew up, with great ease, a very elaborate rule. In due time the Congregation of the Holy Heart of Mary was founded, and the work of the Missionaries began.

One has but to read the letters of Ven. Libermann and of his first companions to see the place held by the Holy Heart of Mary in their spiritual life.

Later on, the Missionary Society of the Holy Heart of Mary was merged into the Congregation of the Holy Ghost, the names of the two Congregations being united in the title —Congregation of the Holy Ghost and of the Immaculate Heart of Mary. The Fathers of the Congregation are working in the west, east and centre of Africa. They are also widespread in the United States where they devote themselves especially to the coloured peoples.

§ IX.

SOCIETIES DEVOTED TO THE HOLY HEART OF MARY. BLESSING OF THE CHURCH ON THEM.

Although the Holy Heart of Mary was revered by holy souls for long centuries, and was publicly and liturgically venerated since the time of St. John Eudes, yet the Venerable Father Libermann seems to have been the first to consecrate a Congregation of Missionary priests to the Holy Heart of Mary, and to mention the Holy Heart in the title of the Congregation. The disciples of Father Libermann, inspired by devotion to the Holy Heart, imitated their spiritual Father.

As early as 1858, we find Monsignor Kobes, C.S.Sp., Bishop of Senegambia, W. Africa, instituting the first Religious Society for native women in Africa, under the title of " Daughters of the Holy Heart of Mary." Those native religious have done great work in the Mission.

Soon after—in 1860—another disciple of Ven. Libermann, Father Delaplace, founded in Paris " The Servants of the Holy Heart of Mary." This Congregation is widely spread in America and Canada. It received the final approbation from Pius X in 1913.[1]

In the Church to-day the Religious Societies which have the Holy Heart of Mary in their title are very numerous.

Let us ask Our Lady to guide and bless all these Congregations so that through them many souls may be drawn to know and love her Holy Heart and the Heart of Jesus.

[1] Such Congregations established in Ireland are:—
    1.—" The Daughters of the Heart of Mary," in the Diocese of Dublin.
    2.—Convent of the Sacred Heart of Mary, Ferrybank, Waterford.
    3.—Convent of the Sacred Heart of Mary, Lisburn.

In 1936 in Nigeria Bishop Heerey founded for natives " The Sisters of the Most Pure Heart of Mary."

CHAPTER III.

MARY, FULL OF GRACE, HUMBLE OF HEART.

" He that is mighty hath done great things to me."
(Luke i. 49.)

INTRODUCTION.

When we consider what God did to the soul of his chosen Mother to prepare her for the ineffable office for which he had selected her, we get some knowledge of her Holy Heart. In the light of God's choice we can see, with certainty if not clearly, something of the glorious beauty of her soul.

Speaking of herself Our Blessed Lady says:

" He that is mighty hath done great things to me."[1]

What were these great things that the Almighty did to Mary?

What exactly did the All-powerful do to the soul of her who was chosen to be the Mother of God made man? Mary, speaking under the impulse of the Holy Spirit, chooses for God the epithet *" mighty."* She does not speak of God as generous, or loving, but as powerful, because what he did to her was a manifestation of his absolute power over all things. What precisely was this " great thing " God did to Mary? What was the great Privilege He gave to His chosen Mother? What God has done to beautify the soul of Mary can be known by God's revelation, which revelation is contained in Scripture and Tradition and has been interpreted for us by the infallible Church. Hence in our study of this beautiful soul, this masterpiece of God's creation, we must look to Holy Church to guide us as regards the details of the work of preparation for the Divine Motherhood.

[1] Luke i. 49.

127

In the Bull which proclaimed the Immaculate Conception of Mary, Holy Church has given us a glorious account of God's work in preparing the soul of his Blessed Mother. From this document we can gather something very definite about the supreme beauty of the Holy Heart of Mary. We can learn the details of what God did to prepare the Heart of Mary for her sublime office as Mother of God.

To fit her for this unique position, God gave her a unique favour, an absolutely sublime privilege. The supreme privilege was this: He kept her heart free from the supreme evil ; He gave her heart the supreme good. He kept her heart, her soul free from sin, and he gave to her heart, to her soul a participation in His own divine nature, He gave her grace, and grace of such perfection and beauty as to be beyond the powers of angels and men to comprehend. This is the favour in which we rejoice when we rejoice in Mary's Immaculate Conception.

The Feast of the Immaculate Conception is a day of great joy for all the children of Mary. But all the children of God must also be children of Mary.

" We cannot have God for our Father," says Saint Ephrem, " unless we have Mary as our Mother."

As good children of Mary we should rejoice in her joys as we sorrow in her sorrows.

The Office and the Mass of the Immaculate Conception speak of joy, the note of joy runs through the text—the joy of Mary and the joy of her children. This note of joy is sounded in the words of the Introit:

" I will rejoice greatly in the Lord, and my soul shall be joyful in my God, for He hath clothed me with the garment of salvation and with the robe of justice hath He covered me."

And again in the Gradual, " Thou art the glory of Jerusalem, thou are the joy of Israel, thou art the honour of our people, alleluia, alleluia."

The first means we have of knowing the Holy Heart, the beautiful soul of Mary, is the contemplation of the great things God has done for her. This contemplation leads us to admiration, to reverence, to confidence, to child-like love.

Let us then consider in detail the great things God has done for the Heart of Mary.

ABSENCE OF THE SUPREME EVIL.

When God drew the souls of our First Parents out of nothing, He showed his gracious kindness by bestowing on them priceless favours. The greatest of these favours, and the one from which many others flowed, was the offering to these human creatures of a share in His own eternal and infinite happiness.

This truth tells us of God's kindness, of his generosity, of the adorable and limitless perfections which make Him so lovable. In His kindness He not only wishes His creatures to be happy, He would even open to them His own eternal bliss. He would give to these poor human creatures nothing less than a participation in the happiness that He Himself enjoys. But how could a creature enter into the joy of God. There was only one way; the creature must be raised to a higher order of being, the creature must in some way be made divine. The work of love God accomplished by giving to Adam and Eve the gift of sanctifying grace, a mysterious participation in his own divine nature. With this supreme gift of sanctifying grace, God gave to Adam and Eve other favours. They were to be preserved from all suffering. They were to be assumed into heaven without passing through the gate of death. They were free from all struggle with unruly passions, for all the passions were ruled without difficulty by the will—this was called the gift of integrity.

All these favours were to be theirs and could be kept by them on one simple condition. The one condition laid down by God was a simple and easy act of obedience.

God's infinite happiness is in His mind and His will, and for man to enter into that bliss it was evidently necessary that man's will should be conformed to the divine will. The easy act of obedience was required of man as a manifestation of this conformity.

We know what happened. Adam ignored the fact that he was a creature, that he was held in existence every moment by the power of God; he wished to be independent of God, which independence was an impossibility, since God was always keeping him in existence. By this breaking of unity of will, Adam ceased to be God's friend, and lost for himself and for his children the favours God had given him. It was a disaster for mankind. We are living under the consequences of Adam's sin. We have to bear suffering and death, we have to struggle against the disorder in our passions. Hence we can win our way to heaven only by the help of God's grace, merited for us by Our Saviour God and Man.

The glory of God's mercy shone out even at the very moment when Adam and Eve learnt the consequences of sin. God promised them a Redeemer and said to the tempter:

" I will put enmities between thee and the woman, and thy seed and her seed ; she shall crush thy head."

Mary was the promised woman. In order that she, through her Son, might crush the head of the Serpent, God on account of the merits of her Divine Son kept her free from sin. This preservation from sin is called the Immaculate Conception. The doctrine of the Immaculate Conception was contained in the Salutation of the Angel Gabriel: " Hail, full of Grace."

The Fathers of the Church in the years that followed the close of the Roman Persecutions, in the fourth and fifth centuries, were most eloquent in writing of Our Lady, of the beauty of her soul, of her freedom from every stain of sin. Extracts from their writings are read in the present office of the Feast of the Immaculate Conception.

§ I.

THE WORDS OF THE EARLY FATHERS.

The Fathers of the Church, writing as early as the fourth and fifth centuries—soon after the close of the great Roman persecutions—tell of the glories of Mary. No epithet is too grand, no phrase too sublime with which to salute the Mother of God. Praises pour from their lips like an impetuous torrent ; epithet piles on epithet, phrase upon phrase, the whole rising majestically heavenward like the paean of some seraph choir.

In the fourth century St. Ephrem, " the harp of the Holy

Spirit," extolled the Mother of God in streams of the sweetest and most melodious eloquence. The following extract is from a prayer to Our Lady.

St. Ephrem, Deacon of Edessa in Asia Minor, A.D. 337.

"Most Holy Lady, alone most pure in soul and body, alone exceeding all in perfection of purity, in chastity and virginity —alone made in thine entirety, the home of the graces of the Most Holy Spirit—hence in purity and sanctity of soul and body, excelling beyond compare, even the angelic virtues, cast thine eyes upon me, my most Holy Lady, Mother of God, full of grace; glory of the nature that is ours in common; Dispenser of all good things; after the Trinity, the Mistress of all; after the Paraclete, another Counsellor, after the Mediator, the whole world's Mediatrix; than Cherubim and Seraphim higher, beyond the power of words to tell, and more glorious by far; unsearchable Abyss of God's goodness; Protection of the universe; Fulness of the grace of the Trinity; holding as it were the second place after the Trinity; Bridge of the whole world leading us to the heights of heaven; Key introducing us to Heaven. . . . ."

(Precationes ad Deiparam. Opp. Graeco-Lat. III, pp. 524-537).

The eloquence of St. Ephrem in praise of the Virgin is echoed by another voice of the fourth century, that of St. Epiphanius:

"What shall I say or what shall I prophesy of the holy and illustrious Virgin? For, God alone excepted, she is greater than all; more beauteous by nature than Cherubim or Seraphim or the entire angel host. No tongue of heaven or earth nor even that of angels can worthily sing her praises. O blessed Virgin! O Dove most pure and Spouse divine! O Mary, Heaven, Temple, Throne of the Divinity, thou possessest Christ, the radiant Sun of heaven and earth. O brightest Cloud, thou hast led from heaven the dazzling Lightning, Christ, to illuminate the world. Hail full of grace, Gate of Heaven, of whom the prophet of the Canticles in prayer, manifestly and openly declares: 'A garden enclosed is my sister, my spouse; a garden enclosed, a fountain sealed up.'"

"She is the Immaculate Lily who bore Christ the unfading Rose. O Holy and Immaculate Mother of God, thou who gavest birth to the Word Incarnate, the Christ the Lamb! O Most Holy Virgin, who didst hold the angelic hosts in awe ; for it is an astounding miracle in the heavens, the woman clothed with the sun ; it is an astounding miracle in the heavens, the woman bearing the light in her arms ; it is an astounding miracle in the heavens, that other cherubic throne ; it is an astounding miracle in the heavens, the Son of the woman, who is both her Father and the Father of ages ; it is an astounding miracle in the heavens, the bridal chamber of the Virgin, having within the Son of God ; it is an astounding miracle in the heavens, the Lord of Angels become the child of a Virgin."

(S. Epiph. de Laudibus B.V.M. Lesson of Matins, 16th Dec.)

With praises no less ardent St. Cyril of Alexandria addresses the Holy Mother of God in his great " Encomium " delivered in A.D. 431 at the Council of Ephesus which proclaimed the doctrine of the divine Maternity of Mary, at that time attacked by the heresiarch Nestorious.

"Hail Mary, of all things in the world most precious.

"Hail Mary, Mother of God. It is thanks to thee that the Shepherds chanted with the Angels, 'Glory to God in the highest and peace on earth to men of goodwill.'

"Hail Mary, Mother of God, it is thanks to thee that the Wise Men brought their Gifts, guided by the Star.

"Hail Mary, Mother of God, it is thanks to thee that the Glorious College of the Apostles was chosen by the Saviour.

"Hail Mary, Mother of God, it is thanks to thee that the Baptist leaped in his Mother's womb, and that the torch was lowered before the Light that never can be extinguished.

"Hail Mary, Mother of God, it is through thee that the ineffable kindness of our God, of which the Apostle tells, has appeared amongst men.

"Hail Mary, Mother of God, it is from thee that has appeared the true Light, who says of Himself: 'I am the Light of the World.'

"Hail Mary, Mother of God, it is thou who didst give birth to the conqueror of death and hell.

"Hail Mary, Mother of God, it is thou who hast placed in this world its Creator and Redeemer, our Guide to the Kingdom of Heaven.

"Hail Mary, Mother of God, it is by thee that every faithful heart is saved.

"We salute thee, O treasure worthy of veneration, that belongest to all mankind. Crown of virginity! Sceptre of orthodoxy!

Temple that can never be destroyed!

Place of Him who is not held by place!

"We salute thee, Mary, Mother of God."

(Encomium ad Deip.)

These words of the Saints regarding the glories of Mary remind us of the words spoken by the Holy Mother of Jesus herself under the inspiration of the Holy Ghost. The idea of Mary's perfect preservation from everything that displeased God was ever prominent through all the centuries. But God reserved the solemn definition of the Immaculate Conception for our time. The doctrine was defined in 1854. Four years later, in 1858, at Lourdes, Our Lady manifested how pleasing the definition was to her. A great wave of joy swept through the Catholic world at this definition. It woke up devotion to Our Lady, a devotion that was slumbering in some souls. It inaugurated a period in the history of the Church characterised by the glory of Mary, the Queen of Heaven, the queen of the whole world. The spiritual effect of the definition was very striking. In the midst of the nineteenth century the danger to the Faith was materialism, which is the denial of the soul, the spiritual principle in man. This implied the denial of man's heavenly destiny, of the life of grace, of the effects of sin on the soul. This materialism was condemned and counteracted by the solemn definition of a great spiritual doctrine. The Immaculate Conception spoke of the Spiritual soul, of the value and beauty of grace, of the effects of sin, of the work of our Redeemer. And as a result, we can say that by the end of the century, Materialism, as a real danger, was dying or dead.

This shows how opportune was the definition and why it was delayed until our time.

THE PRESENCE OF THE SUPREME GOOD.

We have sketched the first aspect of the great things that the mighty God did for Mary from the first moment of her existence. This first aspect was her preservation from all sin, from original sin and from actual sin.

We can, in some way at least, bring home to ourselves the favour given to the soul of Our Lady when she was preserved from the supreme evil which is sin. We ourselves know something of sin, we know the consequences of sin, we feel them every hour of the day, and hence we, with the whole Catholic world, can rejoice with our Queen because we know from what she was preserved.

When we come to consider the second aspect, the treasures of grace which beyond all measure enriched and beautified the Holy Heart of Mary, we are entering into the contemplation of a divine action far above the grasp of any human mind. Here we must hesitate in the very choice of words by which we would try to describe a glory which is all divine.

Fortunately we have the words of the infallible Church in the Bull " Ineffabilis Deus " which give us some idea of the beauty and the glory of the Holy Heart of Mary.

These words we must ponder.

All Mary's graces were a consequence of her Divine Maternity. For this office God selected her. Holy Church in the Bull draws the conclusion saying:

" Wherefore He enriched her, so wonderfully far and away beyond all the angelic spirits and all the saints, with the plenitude of every celestial favour drawn from the treasury of the Divinity, that she, entirely free as she always was from every stain of sin, and all beautiful and perfect, presented such a full measure of innocence and sanctity, that a greater than it, under God, is not understood, and no one except God can even in thought comprehend."

And Holy Church developed the conclusion.

" The most glorious Virgin, for whom He Who is powerful has affected great things, shone forth with a plenitude of celestial gifts, and such an abundance of grace, and with such purity, as to stand forth a miracle which could not be described coming from the hands of God ; nay, the centre and sum of all other miracles—a mother worthy even of God Himself ; and taking into account the condition of created nature, that she approached, as far as possible, the nearest of all other beings, as well angelic as human, to God Himself, so that she soars far above the highest possible praise that can be bestowed upon her."

" She is the abode of all the graces of the Holy Ghost, and with the exception of God alone, she is superior to all created beings—fairer, and more beauteous, and more holy than even the Cherubim and Seraphim and the entire host of angels ; so great is she, that to proclaim her praises fully, the tongues of the heavenly hosts and of all mankind on earth are entirely inadequate."

These solemn declarations of Holy Church give expression to the truth that the Blessed Mother of Jesus was preserved not only from sin but also from every stain of actual sin even the smallest ; and moreover that she was preserved from any struggle with unruly passions—she had the gift of integrity which had been lost by our first parents.

It is a special joy for the children of Mary to know that the Blessed Mother had no struggle with temptation, a struggle of which we all know the bitterness.

This leads us to a still more affectionate act of congratulation and of gratitude to God, and of further admiration when we think in our own limited way of the glory—which we cannot picture—of Mary from the richness of the grace she received.

The words of the Church give us some help here. They express the constant tradition of the Church. But we cannot realise how great is the glory of Mary, we can only rejoice that it is so great that God who is all powerful has done such things for His own Mother. All the glory and beauty bestowed on the Mother of Jesus at the first moment of her existence leads us the children of men, to look up to her and to confide in her who has been appointed a spiritual mother to us also. Hence the Church addresses to us these words: "Let all our dear children of the Catholic Church hear these words from us, and let them with increased zeal in the ways of piety, devotion and love, continue to honour, invoke, and petition the most Blessed Virgin Mary, Mother of God, conceived without sin; and in all dangers, difficulties, necessities, and in occasions of doubt and trial, let them with all confidence have recourse to this sweetest Mother of Mercy and Grace. For nothing is to be feared, nothing to be despaired of, when she leads the way, when she guides our course, when she is favourably disposed, when she stretches her protecting hand—she who bears the heart of a mother towards us and in treating the business of our salvation, has a feeling of solicitude for the whole human race; she is constituted the Queen even of heaven and of earth by our Lord, and she stands, exalted above all the choirs of angels and the ranks of saints, at the right hand of her only-begotten Son, Our Lord Jesus Christ, and she with the entreaties of a mother most powerful pleads our cause—she obtains, too, whatever she asks, and she cannot be disappointed."

When we contemplate the Holy Heart of Mary and think of her twofold privilege, absence of the supreme evil and presence of the supreme good, we can indeed congratulate her, and our congratulation is an act of love. We can rejoice in her glory, in the great things which He that is mighty has done to her.

PRAYER.

O Lord Jesus Christ, our Mediator with the Father, Who hast been pleased to appoint the Most Blessed Virgin, Thy Mother, to be our Mother also and our Mediatrix with Thee, mercifully grant that whosoever cometh to Thee, asking Thy favours may rejoice to receive all of them through her. Amen.

(1) Our Lord Himself has said "Out of the abundance of the Heart the mouth speaketh."[1] We can know the Holy Heart of Mary, we can get a view of her Holy Soul, by considering the words she spoke. Several of Mary's utterances are recorded by the Holy Ghost in the Gospels. Let us be-

---

[1] Matt xii. 34.

gin then by examining her first recorded words—those spoken to the Angel Gabriel. These words reveal her Holy Heart in a marvellous and complete way.

In studying the Holy Heart of Mary, we must ever keep in mind that Our Lady co-operated so perfectly with the special actual graces God gave her, that she never committed any sin no matter how small. Her mind was so enlightened by God, her will was so perfectly united to his Holy Will that she never made a spiritual mistake. She never had to retrace her steps, she never had to correct her spiritual views. She never needed a retreat, her whole soul was ever set towards God, her Holy Heart was always pleasing to Him.

No doubt she understood things better as the years passed by and actual grace followed on actual grace ; but she never had to change or readjust her spiritual attitude before God.

One very important consequence follows from the un-changed direction of her Holy Heart to God. If we were favoured with a view of her Holy Heart on one occasion of her life, if we could penetrate for one moment into the secret of the attitude of her soul in regard to God, we would have got a knowledge of the way she lived, of the spirit in which she met all the events of her life.

Now God in His goodness has given us in the words of Mary, recorded by the Holy Ghost, a clear vision of her beauti-ful soul at the supreme moment of her life—the moment of the Incarnation.

If we examine the words, and penetrate into and explore their full meaning, we shall reach a knowledge of the Heart of Mary; we shall find the secret of Mary, we shall discover the hidden springs of her spiritual life, the great principles that ever directed her.

§ II.

The moment the Archangel stood before Our Lady was indeed the supreme moment of all time, for the Incarnation is the supreme event of all time.

It was the supreme event in the life of Mary. All the wonderful things that God had already done to her were done in preparation for this supreme moment. For this moment God had directed, as we have seen, the preparation of her body and her heart, through a long series of ancestors, so that that Heart might be perfect and not unworthy of giving its life-blood to God. For this moment God had beautified her soul by the glory of the grace given her in her Immaculate Conception. For this moment He had poured a continual stream of actual graces on her beautiful soul, so that every thought, and desire and every act might be absolutely perfect and thus merit an increase of her sanctifying grace, which implied an increase in her glorious beauty in God's eyes. And Mary had co-operated so perfectly with this actual grace, that the design of God for the beautifying of her soul had not been in the least way frustrated, but had been perfectly accomplished.

But throughout all this Mary remained unchanged in her attitude towards God. She knew with ever greater clearness that all she had was God's gift, that God was everything and she was nothing, that He was the Creator, she the creature upheld above nothingness by His Almighty power. And hence we can understand her surprise and her trouble at the salutation of the angel—" Hail full of grace, the Lord is with Thee, Blessed are thou among women."[2] This surprise, this trouble of Mary's soul is recorded in the Gospel.

She, perhaps, was accustomed to visits of the Angels, as many of the saints were accustomed to them. But this visit was different. Hitherto there had been no such reverent salutations as Gabriel now addressed to her.

When he spoke her realisation of her creaturehood was so clear that the titles addressed to her troubled her soul, and she asked herself what was the meaning of this salutation.

The Angel understood her trouble " Fear not, Mary,"[3] the divine messenger reassured her. And then he unfolded to her the glories of the Divine plan. The promised Saviour was to be her Son, He was to be the Son of God, He was to reign for ever, and of His Kingdom there would be no end.

It was a proposal calculated to unbalance any human heart ; but the Holy Heart of Mary, clearly conscious of her creaturehood and of God's care for her, was not unbalanced, but in that moment, sounded deeper depths of her profound humility.

[2] Luke i. 28.
[3] Luke i. 30.

She was to be a mother, so the angel said. She thought of her desire and determination to remain a virgin, which desire she knew was known to God ; and now this most prudent virgin asked God's messenger how God's plan in her regard would be carried out. Then St. Gabriel opened to Mary more completely the secrets of the divine goodness. She was to become a mother by the power and operation of the Holy Ghost. " Behold," he said " The Holy Ghost shall come upon thee, and the power of the most High shall overshadow thee, and therefore the Holy One also which shall be born of thee shall be called the Son of God."[4]

The soul of Mary had been illuminated by the brilliant light of the glorious graces of the Immaculate Conception, and was further illumined by the increase of grace which came with her every act. This increase was beyond all our understanding because of her sanctity and her perfect co-operation.

Mary penetrated into the depths of the divine plan. Her grace-illumined mind saw and understood the long chain of revelations which gave details of the promised Saviour ; she saw the divine goodness manifested in all these details, in particular she understood the Scripture which spoke of the Man of Sorrows. She understood how far God's love for men would lead Him in this way of pain, and how as the Saviour's Mother, she was to enter into His life.

But she was a creature, by the divine power she had been drawn out of nothing ; by that same divine power she was preserved every moment and thus prevented from falling back into the original nothingness from which God had drawn her. She was then the absolute property of the most lovable God, and hence the Divine Will was everything to her. She loved this Divine Will which is identical with God Himself.

Hence from the abundance of her holy heart came the words :

" I am the born woman slave of the Lord,
" Let Him do to me as He wills."

These words of Our Lady were recorded by St. Luke in Greek.[5] The Greek words were inspired by the Holy Ghost,

[4] Luke i. 35.
[5] Original Text. Luke i. 38.

and hence are absolutely exact. The Greek word (doule) means a woman who was born in slavery—not a woman who was reduced to slavery, but a woman who from her first moment was a slave.

These words, these profound and most truthful words reveal to us the Holy Heart of Mary. Her beautiful soul is set before us flooded with the light of truth, so that even we sinners can see into its depths of holiness and understand clearly the secret of the sanctity of Mary, the secret of how she co-operated with God's grace.

The secret is simple.

Mary never lost her grasp of the all-fundamental truth that God is everything and man is nothing. God is the one independent being. Man is essentially a dependent being.

She saw clearly that she was a finite being, dependent for existence at each moment on the most lovable Creator. Her beautiful mind recognises this—" I am the willing slave of the Lord "—and her loving will united itself to the will of the all-lovable Creator—" Let Him do to me all he pleases."

Thus humility opened the soul of Mary to the Divine Action. " The Word was made flesh." The humble Heart of Mary Immaculate knew the supreme joy of the Divine Motherhood.

These words reveal her humility for humility is the loving acceptance of our position as creatures and the shaping of our conduct according to this truth. " Humility," says St. Thomas, " consists in this, that a man keeps to his own place and does not reach out to things above him, but is subject to his superior." (S.C.G. IV, 55).

Mary's humility was most pleasing to God because it was truth. Her humility opened the soul of Mary to the Divine action as our humility opens our soul and prevents us from opposing the action of God in us. Mary knew this, and hence in her Magnificat she tells us how the Lord looked on the humility of His handmaid and did great things to her.

Our humility, our willing recognition of our position as creatures—knowing our place and keeping in it—is the foundation of our spiritual life. To live as affectionate, obedient children of God, guided by His Will, and accepting His cross, this is humility and holiness as far as we are concerned.

Humility appears especially in obedience to those who have authority from God. In Mary's case it appeared in her obedience to St. Joseph. In this she is a model for all Christians, for every one is dependent in some way on fellow creatures.

After the Nativity, the visit of the Shepherds sent by the Angels of heaven manifested Our Lady's glory. The visit of the Kings from the distant East did the same. They found the Holy Child enthroned in the bosom of Mary, and falling down they worshipped, and opening their treasures, they gave most precious gifts.

St. Joseph falls into the shadow in these pictures; he was only the guardian, the foster-father of the Divine Babe. But St. Joseph, as the husband of Mary, was head of the Holy Family. It is in the order of Divine Providence that the husband is the head and ruler of every family.

Obedience to St. Joseph was characteristic of Jesus and Mary. St. Paul compares the position of the husband as head of the family, to the position of Christ as Head of the Church. (Eph. v. 22-25). " Let women be subject to their husbands as to the Lord ; because the husband is head of the wife: as Christ is Head of the Church. Therefore as the Church is subject to Christ, so also let the wives be to their husbands in all things. Husbands love your wives as Christ loved the Church and delivered Himself up for it."

When a Divine command was given to the Holy Family, God acted according to His own law and hence He sent His Angel, not to Mary, but to St. Joseph. The Magi came from Jerusalem in the evening, and an angel came that very night to warn them not to return to Herod. At the same time an angel gave God's command to St. Joseph to " take the Child and His Mother and fly into Egypt and be there until I shall tell thee. For it will come to pass that Herod will seek the Child to destroy Him."[6]

The humility of Mary appears in her obedience to St. Joseph. She obeyed him as God's representative, although he was less wise, and less holy than she was.

It was a difficult obedience—to rise and take the Holy

[6] Matt. ii. 13.

Child and fly away to Egypt, an unknown pagan land by a way unknown to her, and to do this at once, that very night. But Mary's obedience, Mary's perfect humility rose above all difficulties, all obstacles, and now from the depths of the humble Heart of Our Mother there arises again her perfect prayer:

> " I am the born woman slave of the Lord,
> " Let Him do to me as He wills."[7]

[7] Original Text. Luke i. 38.

CHAPTER IV.

MARY BLESSED AMONG WOMEN.

"Come over to Me all you who desire Me and be filled with My fruit."
(Eccles. xxiv.)

INTRODUCTION.

We have contemplated the great things God did for his Holy Mother—her Immaculate Conception, the glory of her graces, the humility, the absolute beauty of her heart.

All God did for Mary was for a purpose—to prepare her for the Divine Motherhood and to prepare her to be a Mother to men. To know how good, how tender, how patient is her maternal heart, her beautiful soul, we shall contemplate what was said by those who were permitted to see in some way into the divine secrets—the angels, the saints, the ordinary faithful. They all will call her blessed.

We can consider the circumstances of each one of those salutations.

I.

The Blessedness of Mary: Her threefold blessedness.

It is very significant that in the Sacred Scripture, the Holy Spirit puts before us the privileges of His Chosen Bride. He does not do so all at once, lest we might fail to sound fully their depths, but He unfolds them one by one, so as to invite us to consider each of them, and like the Blessed Mother herself, to keep the words in our hearts pondering them.

Three times in the Gospel is Our Lady saluted with the title of Blessed: by an angel, by a saint, and by one of the simple faithful. Thus her own prophecy: "Behold all generations shall call me blessed "[1] was verified even in the time of her early life.

[1] Luke i. 48.

Mary was called " blessed " first by *St. Gabriel,* the angel of the Incarnation. His words were the words of God, for the Sacred Scripture tells us that he was sent by God.

Secondly, Mary was called " blessed " by *St. Elizabeth,* and here again the Sacred Scripture tells us explicitly that the saint spoke by the inspiration of the Holy Ghost—" And Elizabeth was filled with the Holy Ghost and she cried out with a loud voice saying " blessed art thou....."[2]

Finally Mary was called "blessed" by the *unknown woman in the crowd,* a type of God's hidden servants, who will never be known here below, but who are saints and most dear to God. We do not know who spoke these words, but we look up to her now in the glory of heaven before the thrones of Jesus and Mary, and no doubt she spoke as did Gabriel and El zabeth at the inspiration of the Holy Ghost.

The Angel then, was the first to salute Mary with the title of " blessed." He spoke of the blessedness she then possessed, of her plenitude of grace. "Hail! full of grace! The Lord is with thee! *Blessed art thou amongst women!* "[3]

She was indeed blessed at that moment in the stupendous glory of her Immaculate Conception, her absolutely unshared privilege since the Fall. She was blessed in the spotless innocence of her life since that first moment. She was blessed in the perfection of her acts of virtue. She was blessed in the immeasurable graces that were the reward of that innocence and that virtue; she was blessed in the intimacy of the dwelling of God in her soul.

Truly, she was blessed among women!

Later on St. Elizabeth poured forth her thoughts to Mary and called her " blessed." This time there was a new privilege, there was a new source of blessedness, and St. Elizabeth indicates it, saying: " *Blessed is the fruit of thy womb.*"[4] She repeats the words of the angel, and adds a new privilege. Yes indeed, a new blessedness, a blessedness to be thought of with childlike joy and reverence. Mary was the living temple of God Incarnate. Her intimacy with Him was greater than even the angelic mind could have conceived. And to be inti-

---

[2] Luke i. 41-42.
[3] Luke i. 28.
[4] Luke 1. 42.

mate with Jesus is joy and contentment, repose and peace. This was Our Lady's new blessedness. It was the blessedness of Nazareth.

Was there any other further blessedness that could be hers? Could she desire anything further? Yes! there was a further blessedness, and the Holy Spirit puts it before us in the words of the unknown woman who seeing and hearing Jesus, cried out: "*Blessed is the womb that bore thee, and the breasts that gave Thee suck.*"

This unknown woman repeats the thought of St. Elizabeth —" Blessed is the womb that bore thee "; and she adds a new source of blessedness saying: " Blessed are the breasts that gave Thee suck."[5] Blessed art thou in thy maternal ministrations. Blessed are thou in thy loving care of the Holy Child. Blessed are thou in every mark of motherly affection thou didst show Him. Blessed art thou in the giving of thyself to Him. Blessed art thou in the work of building up the Sacred Body of God made man.

It was the blessedness of Bethlehem.

Our Lady was indeed blessed in bearing Jesus in her womb, in giving Him her life-blood, in ministering to Him of her very substance. But she could still desire to see Him, to minister to Him by the very act of her will, and to give Him of herself by her own deliberate and conscious free act.

In Bethlehem this blessedness was hers. For there she saw Him before her. She ministered to Him. She watched over Him with sweet solicitude. She bore Him in her arms with profoundest reverence. She poured out all her heart in her maternal caresses. She gave of her very self to Him. By her ministrations, she strengthened, she built up the Sacred Body of God made Man. And she saw Him growing stronger and taller as the months passed.

To see Jesus and to minister to Him was then the blessedness of Bethlehem, and this blessedness was the object of Mary's desire and expectation ; and the Church puts all this before us in the feast of the Expectation of the Blessed Virgin celebrated eight days before Christmas.

[5] Luke xi. 27.

II.

We are invited to contemplate the Blessedness of Mary in Bethlehem. The Holy Spirit puts the Blessedness of Bethlehem before us.

Everything in the Sacred Scripture was written under divine inspiration, nothing was written by chance. And as the words relating to the Blessed Virgin are not many, but indicate much, each of them should be the subject of our loving thought. When the Holy Spirit inspired the Evangelist to record the words of the unknown woman in the crowd, He placed before us a picture of Mary's blessedness in Bethlehem and invited us to contemplate this particular blessedness which seems to crown and complete the others.

Consider for a moment the innumerable things that might have been recorded in the Scripture regarding the Blessed Mother of Jesus, how many details of her long life, how many words spoken by her, how many words spoken to her and about her, all these we would long to know. And yet of all these possible texts of inspired Scripture the Holy Spirit has selected only a few. These few have been selected for the glory of His chosen Spouse and set before us as material for our loving meditation on Bethlehem.

The Church recalls the Mother in Bethlehem.

If we seek the mind of the Church, as expressed in her Christmas offices, on Mary's blessedness in Bethlehem, we cannot but be struck by the way she re-echoes the words of the woman in the crowd. In fact she uses no other words to put before us the glory of the Mother in her maternal privileges. As we have seen above, the glory of Mary comes from her nearness to Jesus. And in this first part of Our Lord's life her intimacy with Him is simply overwhelming in its awfulness, while her glory absolutely dazzles us. Intimacy appears in all her maternal duties ; in her constant motherly care for the Holy Babe ; in her support for His infantine weakness ; in her tenderness in every touch ; in her outpouring of maternal affection.

The Church leaves to the devout contemplation of her

children the consideration of all these separate glories of Mary. In the Office she wishes to sum them all up in one word and for this she naturally selects the words of the unknown woman which were chosen by the Holy Spirit to be recorded in the Gospel. Thus in the Matins of Christmas Day in the responses of the third Nocturn, she cries out:

" Blessed be the womb of the Virgin Mary which bore the Son of the Eternal Father, and blessed the bosom that gave milk to Christ the Lord."

And in the hymn of Lauds she reminds us that Jesus who feeds the birds of the air was Himself fed with a little milk ;

" Et lacte modico pastus est, per quem nec ales esurit."

And again in the Office of the Octave of Christmas she comes back to the same thought: *" Regem angelorum sola virgo lactabat ubere de coelo pleno."* To the King of the Angels the Virgin alone gave milk of a bosom repleted by heaven.

And in the Office of the Holy Family during the octave of the Epiphany, the Vesper hymn repeats the same idea:

" Maria, dives gratia,

O sola quae casto potes
Fovere Jesum pectore,

Cum lacte donans oscula."

" O Thou whose bosom nursed Him!
O Mary highly graced!
O Thou whose breast gave milk to Jesus,
Whose arms Thy God embraced."

And once again in the hymn at Lauds of the Feast of the Purification of Our Lady, we read:

O Gloriosa Virginum .
Sublimis inter sidera,
Qui te creavit parvulum
Lactente nutris ubere.

O glorious maid enthroned on high!
Above the lights that deck the sky,
O Maid at whose maternal breast
Thy Infant Maker fed caressed.

What incomprehensible Glory and ineffable joy are set before us in these words of the Liturgy!

The glory of Mary, the Mother of the Most High, is truly the glory of the woman, who, as the Scripture says, was clothed in the dazzling glory of the sun!

And of this glory she herself spoke saying: —

"Because He that is mighty hath done great things to me . . . For behold from henceforth All generations shall call me blessed."[6]

The Lovers of God have contemplated the Mother in the same way.

The Saints and servants of God, in imitation of the Church, have loved to contemplate the Blessed Mother ministering to Jesus in Bethlehem; they loved to think of the Holy Child enthroned in her heart, supported by her loving arms, caressed with her tender affection.

They preserved and increased their own devotion to the Mother of Jesus by these contemplations; and they encouraged a like devotion among the faithful by their writings, and by promoting the use of pictures and statues of the Blessed Mother with the Holy Child in her arms.

St. Alphonsus Liguori, a great lover of Our Lady, thus writes of her blessedness in Bethlehem:

" Consider the devotion, the tenderness, the love which Mary felt on seeing in her arms and on her bosom the Lord of the world, the Son of the Eternal Father, who had deigned to become her son, choosing her from among all women to be His Mother. Mary, now holding Him to her bosom, adores Him as God; kissing His feet as her King, and then His face as her Son."

And the saintly Father Laval, the Apostle of Mauritius, another great servant of Mary, who consecrated himself to the missions at the altar of Our Lady of Victories, who had her name continually on his lips, entertained and fostered, as appears especially in his letters to the Venerable Libermann, this most tender aspect of devotion to Mary.

[6] Luke i. 48-49.

How did he entertain and foster this tender devotion? We find the secret in what is recorded in his life—" He kept nothing by him except his Bible, his crucifix, some relics and a little oil painting of the Blessed Virgin Mary."

This keeping of an oil painting is significant. It was a picture showing Our Lady with the Holy Child folded in her bosom. This spoke of the blessedness of Our Lady.

We, too, should frequently recall this picture of Mary with the Holy Child in her arms. It is presented to us by the Holy Ghost. Let us contemplate it with reverence and affection. It will help us to cultivate a tender love for our Blessed Mother. It is an easy, true and intelligible source of devotion.

When we try to picture the stable at Bethlehem we have a difficulty owing to the fact that the Scripture gives us little help in details, and also because the pictures we have seen are all so different. But when we picture Jesus enfolded in the arms of His Blessed Mother we know that our picture is correct. We know, too, that the Holy Heart of Mary is the Heart of the Mother of God made Man, the Mother of Jesus Who is the Life of our souls.

> Mother of Christ ; Mother of Christ,
> He was all in all to thee,
> In the winter's cave, in Nazareth's home,
> In the hamlets of Galilee.
> So Mother of Christ, Mother of Christ,
> He will not say nay to thee ;
> When He lifts His face to thy sweet embrace
> Speak to Him, Mother, of me.

"MY SPIRIT HAS REJOICED IN GOD, MY SAVIOUR"

INTRODUCTION.

How immense is the richness of Christmas, richness in touching details, all of which reveal to us the abyss of God's goodness.

A general view of the mysteries of Bethlehem is no doubt sufficient for some souls, but, for most, special meditation on

[7] Luke i. 47.

each point is a great help and leads them most sweetly to advance in the love of Jesus and Mary.

Let us consider in some detail the Blessed Mother's position in the mystery of Bethlehem.

All the glory of Mary arises from her Divine Motherhood. And this glory comes before us in the mystery of Bethlehem more strikingly than in any other mystery.

In Bethlehem we see pictured before us the loving intimacy of the union of Jesus and Mary, and the amazing position of dependence on His Blessed Mother in which Jesus placed Himself.

To *contemplate* this will lead our hearts to *that tender devotion* to the Blessed Mother which is characteristic of all the saints, and to that childlike confidence in her motherly care which God wishes to see in all her children.

III. CONTEMPLATION.

The Joy of Mary in ministering to Jesus.

Let us now consider the joy of the Blessed Virgin in ministering to her Divine Son, in taking care of Him, in watching Him, in the giving of her own self to Him. Let us contemplate her intimate union with Jesus.

To love is to give. Generosity is the natural manifestation of love. He who loves is sweetly drawn to give. To give is a proof of love—not merely the giving of possessions, but the giving of oneself, of one's strength. And giving is also the joy of love, a joy which every lover knows.

This character appears in God's love for us: He gave Himself, He gave His blood, He gave His life, He gives Himself daily in the Most Holy Sacrament.

This giving is the very proof of the reality of His love. And to give Himself was His joy: "I have a baptism," He says, "wherewith I am to be baptised, and how am I straitened until it be accomplished."[8] To suffer in body was even a contentment to His Sacred Heart because it was suffering for those He loved.

[8] Luke xii. 50.

And it was the same with the Blessed Mother of Jesus. To give to Jesus was purest joy. To give to Him of her care, of her devotion, of her strength, of her affection, of her very self was joy unspeakable.

The Dependence of Jesus on Mary, and His desire for Her Loving Care.

Let us now think of the Holy Child. Let us think of Him on the ground, in the straw. Let us contemplate His littleness, and weakness, and His complete dependence on the care of His Blessed Mother.

Let us contemplate His desire for her affectionate care, for her maternal caresses.

The desire of God! The desire of God for a creature's ministrations! What a mystery of abasement! Jesus was little! Jesus was helpless! Jesus was completely dependent on His chosen Mother!

As He lay on the ground His inarticulate infantine cry told of His desire for that Mother's affectionate embrace. The stretching out of His little hands revealed His desire to rest in her loving arms.

It was the desire of God made man. O Adorable mystery! Mary knew the voice of that Infant cry: She lifted up the Infant God: she took Him in her loving arms.

And Jesus is content! It is God finding contentment in the affection His creature can give Him.

The contentment of a babe in a mother's caress is proverbial. But when the Babe is Jesus, and the Mother is Mary, the thought of the contentment is too deep for words.

That God should seek the love of any creature, and find a contentment in it is a mystery that we can never fathom, a mystery that tries our faith. But it is such a revelation of His goodness that we need to realise it. And hence He abased Himself, and we see Him as a helpless human Babe longing for the affectionate care of her whom He had chosen to be His earthly Mother.

From the mystery of the contentment of Jesus in His mother's affection, we naturally pass to the adoration of Mary in contemplating His weakness and dependence on her.

He was God omnipotent and yet He sought support from her arms. He was absolute Beatitude and yet He sought contentment in her caresses.

Her faith in His divinity made her feel most keenly His position of dependence ; His very desire for her affection cast her holy soul into depths of humility.

She felt for His weakness, she felt for His abasement. His dependence deepened the reverence with which she carried Him, and hence every ministration was adoration, while every look was love.

The desire of Jesus for the love which Mary alone could give Him has its counterpart in His mysterious desire for the love which I alone can give Him.

His Sacred Heart thirsts not for my possessions, but for my very self. I alone can satisfy that thirst. His desire is not for souls in general, but it is a desire for my soul. If I do not satisfy Him, His Heart will not be satisfied. His infantine cry for the affectionate caresses of Mary has its counterpart in His great cry from the Cross, in the words: "I thirst."[9] It is for my love He thirsts.

The lifting up of His little hands has its counterpart in the opening wide of His arms on the Cross that told of His desire, of which it is written: " All the day long I have opened wide my hands to those that contradict Me, to those who refused to give themselves to Me."[10] The desire of God is to possess each one of us, and each of us has, by His grace, the power of satisfying that desire.

It is through the Maternal Heart of Mary that we will get the grace to yield ourselves to the sweet appeal of the love of Jesus.

Mary's Vision of the Future. While Mary contemplated the humiliation of Jesus in her arms, while she rejoiced in the giving of herself to Him, *did she see into the future?*

We know that *the angels,* although they have their powers concentrated on the Beatific Vision, can see in God all the things that they desire to see.

If so great a privilege was given to the angels may we not

[9] ixx. 28.

[10] Romans x. 21.

expect that a similar privilege was given to the Queen of Angels?

The *Prophets* were permitted to see into the future. Was this vision not permitted to the Queen of Prophets ?

But apart from such special privileges, surely Mary, the Mother of Jesus, with her unclouded intelligence, could read deep enough in the Divine Scriptures to know that she was preparing the instrument of the world's redemption.

Surely His Holy Mother understood that this precious body she was building up with her constant care, with her affectionate devotion would give untold glory to God, and would finally be inundated with glory and joy in Heaven. And was it not a new and special joy for her to think of that future which awaited in eternity the real Body she nurtured in her arms, the precious Blood which daily increased through her ministrations.

We should see in this aspect of Mary's maternal privilege, in this special joy from her knowledge of the future, *a beautiful figure of our own privileges,* of our own personal blessedness—the blessedness of every child of Holy Church.

Like Mary we are called to give of our devotion, of our strength, of our very being.

We are called to give all this to Jesus. As Mary gave of her very self to build up the real body of Jesus, so we are privileged to give of our strength, of our time, of our very selves, *to build up his Mystical Body;* to co-operate in the making of Saints, to toil for the sanctification first of ourselves, and then of those under our care. For are not both we and they among the members of the Mystic Body of Jesus?

This is true not only of priests, but of parents, of teachers, of all Catholics.

St. Paul tells us how Christ gives to His Church, Apostles, Prophets, Evangelists, Pastors and Doctors (Eph. iv.)

He describes our life work, he speaks of us.

We have the privilege of being sent by the Church in Christ's name—we have to be all these at once, and this whether we work in the missions or in education.

We must be Apostles—we are sent.

We must be Prophets—we are appointed to speak His message.

We must be Evangelists—we are called to spread the Good News of Jesus.

We must be Pastors—we are to be occupied in watchful care of our flock.

We must be Doctors—we are to be learned in spiritual things.

St. Paul then states *the object of this sending.* It was:

(i) For the perfecting of the Saints,

(ii) For the work of the ministry,

(iii) For the building up of the Body of Christ. That is: for the perfecting of the good ; for distributing God's grace to the faithful ; for increasing the numbers and the sanctity of the members of Christ.

The final object of our life work is then the building up of the Mystic Body of Christ. This is an aspect of our life that we should never forget. Like Mary *we can look forward* even to eternity, where we hope to behold the members of the Mystical Body of Jesus that have been built up and perfected by our co-operation with grace.

Nothing of our life *can be lost* if it is consciously directed to this building up of the Body of Jesus. We may not see the results ourselves, but the result will be there even to eternity.

CONCLUSION.

We have contemplated the joy of Mary in Bethlehem, the desire of Jesus for the affectionate care of His Holy Mother, and the eternal fruits of Mary's ministry.

Let us keep these thoughts in our heart, pondering on them. They are all summed up in the picture of the Blessed Mother with the Holy Child folded in her arms.

To advance in the understanding of this Mother's glory, and to keep our devotion to her deep and tender, we must often think of her maternal union with Jesus in Bethlehem as the Holy Spirit suggests to us. (It was thus Fr. Laval thought of Mary and became a saint).

We all know how the Church loves to introduce the Mother of Jesus into her public prayers.

In the Divine Office each day, at the very beginning, she places the *Ave* immediately after the *Pater ;* and at the end, when the work of God, the Opus Dei, is completed she wishes us to go forth with a picture of the Blessed Mother in our minds.

Hence she concludes with one of the antiphons of our Lady, the words of which reveal her devotion to the Blessed Mother.

And then she desires us on bended knee to ask pardon for our faults in the Divine Office, and once again, in the verse of the Sacrosanctae, she brings before us in all her glory the all-holy Mother of Jesus with the Divine Babe enthroned on her Heart.

It is the old picture of the blessedness of Bethlehem, and to recall it, the Church once more re-echoes the words of that unknown woman which spoke of that blessedness.

Beata viscera Mariae Virginis, quae portaverunt aeterni Patris Filium,

Et beata ubera, quae lactaverunt Christum Dominum.

> Oh, blest be Mary's virgin womb
> Which bore the Eternal Father's Word ;
> And also blest her virgin breast
> Which milk did give to Christ the Lord.

Divine Love was the sole moving power of Mary's maternal heart ; that love dominated and directed all her aspirations. Because of her complete co-operation with the fulness of grace that was hers, she was completely responsive to the desires of the Sacred Heart of Jesus. Even as she knew the very heart-beats of her Child, she was uniquely sensitive to every movement of His soul, and so, she shared His all consuming desire to give us abundance of Divine Life. Thus the hearts of Jesus and Mary are one in the activity of love. The Immaculate Heart of Mary longs for souls to be drawn to Jesus. When we seek Him lifted in her arms, she asks Him to draw us to Himself as He promised to do through the merits of His Passion.[11] Thus devotion to the Immaculate Heart of Mary is something more than the comforting thought of her maternity, *it is the practical adoption of the desires of the Hearts of Jesus and Mary,* and in particular ot their desire to draw all souls to a share in the Divine Life. We are re-minded of this by the petitions in the Mass prescribed for

[11] "And I, if I be lifted up from the earth, will draw all things to myself." St. John xii. 32.

the Feast of the Immaculate Heart of Mary. The Church prays "*that our hearts may be enkindled by that divine fire which ineffably inflamed the Heart of the Blessed Virgin*"; and significant is the petition of the Collect—" O, Almighty and Eternal God . . . . . . mercifully grant that we who with devout minds celebrate the festival of the Immaculate Heart *may be able to live according to Thy own Heart.*"

> O Mother of Christ, Mother of Christ
> What shall I ask of thee ?
> I do not sigh for the wealth of earth,
> For the joys that fade and flee.
> But Mother of Christ, Mother of Christ,
> This do I long to see—
> The Bliss untold which thine arms enfold,
> The Treasure upon thy knee.

POINTS FOR PRAYER.

INTRODUCTION.

§ I.—THE BLESSEDNESS OF MARY: HER THREEFOLD BLESSEDNESS. THE BLESSEDNESS OF BEING HER CHILDREN.

§ II.—WE ARE INVITED TO CONTEMPLATE THIS BLESSEDNESS:

   (a) BY THE HOLY SPIRIT.

   (b) BY THE CHURCH.

   (c) BY THE SAINTS.

§ III.—LET US CONTEMPLATE:

   (a) THE JOY OF MARY IN MINISTERING TO JESUS.

   (b) THE DESIRE OF JESUS FOR HIS MOTHER'S CARE AND AFFECTION.

   (c) MARY'S VISION OF THE FUTURE.

CONCLUSION.